Praise for *Once Upon a School*

"Arguably, the most joyful of human experiences is pouring your soul into the lives of those who are fragile and vulnerable or troubled who will have a future because you care—an infant in your arms or a child experiencing homelessness. This page-turner of a narrative tells the story of just such self-giving: a white woman of privilege is inspired to invest her life into the responsibility each of us is assigned—repairing the world, tikkun olam. This is not a story of self-adulation. Mistakes are made; a heart is broken; someone has to begin again. It is, however, a story of redemption, brimming over with hope and light. I heartily recommend it."

—THE REVEREND ED BACON, AUTHOR OF *8 HABITS OF LOVE*

"If you've ever wondered if one person with a dream can spark a revolution, if you've ever wondered how to bounce back after loss, if you've ever wondered if love really does win .... Kate Kennedy's book will give you hope and nudge you to be the change you want to see in the world."

—THE REVEREND CANON STEPHANIE SPELLERS, CANON FOR EVANGELISM AND RECONCILIATION UNDER PRESIDING BISHOP MICHAEL CURRY, AUTHOR OF *THE CHURCH CRACKED OPEN AND THE EPISCOPAL WAY* (WITH ERIC LAW)

"Kate Kennedy takes us into her world as she does the impossible—creates a tuition free private school for children who have experienced homelessness in Atlanta. The 'how' she did it is as fascinating as the "why" she did it. Through her writing and by her example, Kate inspires us all to not just be 'do-gooders' but to be 'change-makers.' *Once Upon a School* encourages us to consider our own call to action on causes that matter and more importantly, take that leap of faith."

—KATHY IZARD, AUTHOR OF THE HUNDRED STORY HOME,
THE LAST ORDINARY HOUR, AND TRUST THE WHISPER

"Kate Kennedy built a school, from scratch, and that's as hard as it sounds. You will laugh, scratch your head, and wonder at how easily things can come together and maybe even more easily, fall apart. More importantly, if you wonder if you can do something that matters in the world, read this book."

—THE REVEREND WINNIE VARGHESE, RECTOR, ST. LUKE'S EPISCOPAL
CHURCH ATLANTA; AUTHOR OF CHURCH MEETS WORLD

"In this compelling book, author Kate Kennedy shares a powerful journey of reflection and growth. As we learn about Kennedy's work to create a school for children experiencing homelessness, we get a front-row view into many of the challenges, blessings and grace that occurred. This book is a brave and powerful narrative, and it is a gift to the reader!"

—KATE H. RADEMACHER, AUTHOR OF RECLAIMING REST: THE PROMISE
OF SABBATH, SOLITUDE, AND STILLNESS IN A RESTLESS WORLD

"*Once Upon a School* is so painfully and beautifully encouraging —a moving look into the common struggles shared by so many families, the stark differences in so many families experiences, and the inequities that lead to far different outcomes. Kate Kennedy takes us on an emotional journey through her story, never hesitating to open her heart and let the reader gaze into the joy and pain inside. Her courage in the face of her fears, along with the failures and successes, combine to open a window into the reader's own journey, inspiring us to take the next step, no matter the consequence. This is a book about hope!"

–THE REVEREND TONY JOHNS,
EXECUTIVE DIRECTOR, CROSSROADS

Once Upon a School

ONCE UPON A SCHOOL

A Story of Dreaming Big,
Falling Hard,
and Bouncing Back

Kate Kennedy

Once Upon a School: A Story of Dreaming Big, Falling Hard, and Bouncing Back
Copyright © 2024 Kate Kennedy

ISBN: 979-8-9899708-0-3 (Paperback); 979-8-9899708-1-0 (E-Book)

Cover illustration: Adobe Stock
Book design by C'est Beau Designs

*For all the dreamers and
change-makers in the world*

May God give you grace not to sell yourself short.
The grace to risk something big for something good.
The grace to remember that the world is now too
dangerous for anything but truth,
and too small for anything but love.

—WILLIAM SLOANE COFFIN, JR.

PROLOGUE

There is no greater agony than bearing an untold story inside of you.

–MAYA ANGELOU

There are moments in your life that define you. Some are big, and some are small. Some are beautiful, and others are painfully bitter. Starting The Boyce L. Ansley School was one of those defining moments for me. At the time, I was just trying to find a new solution to an old problem. It was what I thought needed to be done.

It's tragic that we live in a world where innocent children fall through the cracks of the system simply because they are born into circumstances beyond their control. Generational poverty and educational inequity hijack the potential of so many helpless young students. I'm passionate about exposing this crisis and working to find ways to create paths of opportunity so that children born into poverty can write stories of success beyond their circumstances. Once I recognized the issue, I couldn't sit back and do nothing, and so, I just started—one step at a time.

The school was more than simply a project or a job. The school was and is an extension of me. I look back over my own life, and I clearly see the events and circumstances that led me down this path. Never have I felt God calling me to do something so directly. Building The Ansley School was holy work that came from and fed into my DNA. For a moment, I couldn't see where the school ended, and I began. The families and children entrenched themselves into my heart and my soul.

This book is about my journey. It's about building a school. It's about social justice, but it's also about a woman who tried and failed and found herself in the process. These are my memories, my recollections, and the broadest view I can see from my perspective, but this is more than just my story.

Recently, I learned a newly minted word: "sonder." It means "the realization that each random passerby is living a life as vivid and complex as your own."[1] "Sonder" was coined specifically to describe a universal truth that had yet to be named. No one lives in a vacuum. We are each a player in the bigger story. Our lives connect and intertwine in a million ways. My story is a part of your story, and your story is part of mine, or, at the very least, my story can point to truths in your own story.

While creating the school, I believe that everyone was doing what they thought best for the program and the children. I have done my best to tell the story without judgment. We all tried. Sometimes we succeeded wildly and sometimes we failed miserably. This is not a story of placing blame or pointing fingers. With the exception of the Ansley family, the Stinson family,[2] my family, Crossroads, and St. Luke's Episcopal Church, I have changed all the names.

We were all in the trenches. We were all devoted, and we were all imperfect. No one could have predicted how it would play out, and the story isn't yet complete. For me, the deepest truth is that in the end, it doesn't matter how hard you fall. What's important is how high you bounce. This book shares the saga of testing and trusting the bounce while marveling in gratitude at sonder along the way. This book is about me, but it's also about us.

CHAPTER ONE
Dreaming Big

Reach high for stars lie hidden in your soul.
Dream deep for every dream precedes the goal.

–MOTHER THERESA

It was mid-October 2018. My husband and I were sitting at one of our favorite local pizza restaurants. A pepperoni and mushroom calzone for him and a slice of spinach and mushroom for me (hold the garlic and the extra cheese) and two draft beers. It was after 9 p.m. We were overdressed for the location, but it was one of "our" places—a casual local restaurant we had been coming to for all the years we had lived in Atlanta. After an event like the one we'd been to that night, we needed a moment to celebrate and reflect in an easy, familiar spot.

The restaurant was in a busy part of Atlanta, and from our seats on the patio, the city noises—highlighted with the occasional car horn, siren, or whoop of an exuberant group out on the town—created an energy almost as robust as the thrill I felt inside. I was smiling ear to ear. I just kept repeating the same words:

"This is unbelievable. We actually did it. This may be the best night of my life."

Three and a half years earlier, I had embarked on a wild journey to open a school in Atlanta for children without stable housing. So many people said it couldn't be done. So many people thought I was wasting my time. So many people thought I was in way over my head, yet here we were tonight, my husband and I in our cocktail party attire, eating pizza, drinking beer, and celebrating the reality of The Boyce L. Ansley School—a privately funded tuition-free school for children experiencing homelessness. After years of planning, fundraising, and finding new paths when dead ends and naysayers seemed to persist, we had opened the doors of the school.

Just two months earlier, in August 2018, we had stood in anticipation and awe as a group of four-year-olds—some of whom had spent the previous night on the street—arrived with their parents at their new classroom to meet their new teachers. They were each wearing crisp white shirts with the school logo monogrammed on the pocket, navy blue shorts and skirts, and each was proudly carrying the school bus backpacks with brand-new supplies that had been donated to our inaugural class of scholars. (We intentionally chose to call the children "scholars" because it signifies more than just typical students coming to school. To us, it meant students who are dedicated to growth and learning in all parts of their lives. "Scholar" was a title of respect and admiration for the work they were ready to do.)

My exuberance at the presence of these young children and their families on the first day of school only grew as they continued to return day after day after day to the same classroom in the same building with the same teacher and the same friends. The first two months passed with some twists and turns and unexpected surprises, but our tiny pre-K scholars were growing and learning. And tonight, on a brilliant October evening, we hosted an event that drew more than one hundred of Atlanta's biggest funders who came to celebrate and support this bold project named for the woman who helped me believe in my own ability to make real change in the world.

Boyce Lineberger Ansley, for whom the school is named, was a community legend and one of my trusted mentors. Everything Boyce touched benefited from her enormous heart. She was a firm believer in philanthropy—

not just funding, but giving back her time, her energy, and her wisdom. Her life raised the bar for all. She was a natural leader and instinctive fundraiser. She was charming and relentless as she raised funds for the important causes she championed. It was well-known that an invitation to lunch with Boyce (or Boycie, as she was known to her close friends and family) could be very expensive. You could expect a delightful conversation plus a compelling solicitation for a contribution. Boycie served on and led numerous nonprofit boards both locally and nationally, and she loved to groom young adults to be civic-minded professionals.

In February 2015, as a group from my church bounced along the winding roads of north Georgia on our way to a leadership retreat, I began chatting about my concern that so many children who lacked stable housing seemed to be falling through the cracks of our school systems. For several years, I had been volunteering with homeless-serving agencies in the Atlanta area. I learned very quickly that without stable housing, life is complicated and difficult. The parents I spoke with in shelters and on the streets said that figuring out where their children would sleep each night or where they would find their next meal was more important than worrying about which school they were zoned for or gathering all the necessary paperwork to enroll. And statistically, those who did enroll were falling behind and failing out at numbers much greater than their peers with stable housing.[3]

"What really needs to exist," I said as we drove, "is a special school for children experiencing homelessness. Someone really needs to build one."

"Yes—*you* do need to do that," Boycie exclaimed.

"No, I said *someone*," I quickly responded.

And with a mix of genteel Southern charm and commanding authority that only Boycie could pull off, she said, "*You* said *someone*, but *I* said *you*. If you create this school, I will raise all the money you need to make it a reality."

"Funny, Boycie," I laughed. "Now can we open the Cheetos Puffs you brought?"

It may have been one of my most favorite things about Boycie. She was powerful and refined with perfectly coiffed hair and long, red fingernails—a woman of society in every way—and her favorite snack was Cheetos Puffs.

As we bounced along munching on our snacks and licking the orange dust off our fingers, the conversation in the car moved on to other subjects, but I couldn't help but notice the wave of fear mixed with hope and energy that began to swell in my gut. No one ever said "no" to Boycie. She was a force of nature.

In the end, Boycie's relentless pestering and unwavering support became the catalyst to take the first steps of my journey. Her persistence gave me the push I needed to mold my idea into my dream and my dream into reality. It took a full year from that first conversation, but in the spring of 2016 I began.

A few months into my work, there was a meeting at church that I needed to attend. I considered skipping it because I was so focused on organizing a feasibility study for the school, but in the end, my sense of responsibility won. I tore myself away from my makeshift workspace at home and headed to my meeting. I entered the doors of the church still rolling through plans and lists for the school in my mind when the look on our priest's face stopped me in my tracks.

"Boycie has died," he said.

The information didn't register. How could that be? I knew she had gone into the hospital for a heart procedure, but it never occurred to me that she wouldn't survive. The news quickly spread. Her sudden death sent shock waves through the community. She was truly a beacon of power and love and strength for everyone she met. Boycie personified the power of women to make lasting and meaningful impact in the world. I knew then that I had to keep going. She believed in me, and if Boycie believed you could succeed she was usually right.

With Boycie in my corner, I had been certain of one thing: she *would* raise all the money we needed to open and run the school. That had been her declaration to me, and there was no doubt in my mind that she could do it without blinking an eye. When Boycie got behind a cause or a plan, she could move mountains to ensure its success. Boycie had been my greatest cheerleader. Without her by my side, I wasn't sure if I could make this happen.

Then it came to me. What if we named the school after Boycie? I wanted children to go to a school with a name that carried some gravitas. Boycie's name would offer that. I also knew that Boycie's name might help bring in some supporters who she would have reached out to for funding. Plus, and maybe most importantly, I needed the constant reminder that Boycie believed in me and in this project. I was confident that she was smiling down on this epiphany of mine.

I reached out to Boycie's husband, Shepard Ansley, and invited him to lunch with our small planning committee. Shepard is a wonderful man. A successful Atlanta attorney in a firm started by his grandfather, he is kind, approachable, and always wears a smile on his face. Shepard and Boycie were a lovely and influential couple in so many ways. Always up for a social engagement, Shepard accepted our invitation. We met at a quaint French bistro near midtown Atlanta.

The day of our meeting was beautiful. The weather was perfect. The restaurant was quiet and subtly upscale. I ordered Croque Monsieur (one of my favorites) and an iced tea. After our drinks arrived, I began the conversation.

"So, Shepard, I bet you're wondering why we invited you here today."

"Well, yes," he said. "I must admit I'm a little curious."

Shepard hadn't been aware of my conversations with Boycie about the idea of creating a school, but as I explained the issue and the plans, Shepard was quick to jump on board.

"That sounds like Boycie," he said. "She always got behind a good idea, and she could be very persuasive. Thanks for sharing this story with me and thanks for moving forward with this project. I'll help in any way I can."

"Well, we have a favor to ask you. We were wondering if we could name the school after Boycie."

And before we could even go into the reasons why we thought this was a good idea, he smiled and said, "Absolutely. What an honor."

I finally took a bite of my sandwich, relieved at his enthusiasm and energized to move forward. I wasn't sure exactly what The Boyce L. Ansley School would look like, but I knew we were on our way. Any fear I had about the project was overshadowed by the joy I felt at this first step. I wish Boycie could have been with us to guide and support and encourage, but I felt her presence, and it offered me hope and energy.

More than a year later, when the school was truly becoming a reality, I visited Shepard in the beautiful home where he and Boycie had raised their children and entertained so many. He wanted to show me something he thought I might like. On the coffee table in his living room sat a cardboard shoebox filled with hundreds of index cards. Shepard explained that this was his system for thanking people who had reached out with condolences. Each handwritten three-by-five-inch lined index card in Shepard's elegant cursive held a name, contact information, and what was offered as condolence—a meal, a note, a gift, a donation, and so on.

"I thought you might like to see all the people who reached out after Boycie died. She was so loved. I think these friends would be interested in hearing about the school you're building in her name."

He explained that he would like to think of a way to let them know. And with that conversation, an idea began to blossom. The school was scheduled to open in August. What if we invited all these friends to a special event to honor Boycie's legacy?

Tonight, less than three years after my initial conversation with Boycie and only two months after the launch of the school, our small but mighty team had successfully pulled off that very event. It was a glorious evening held in the beautiful atrium of The Center for Puppetry Arts—another of Boycie's favorites. The use of the venue had been donated to us for the event by the Center in honor of their friend Boyce Ansley. The open, two-story space had been filled not only with photographs and looping video of the amazing scholars who made up the inaugural class of The

Boyce L. Ansley School, but also so many of Boycie's friends and family who had come to celebrate her life and legacy and the successful opening of a groundbreaking program for children experiencing homelessness. As I walked to the podium at the top of the central open staircase, I looked with awe over the crowd of people. I was filled with wonder at all that we had accomplished and a powerful sense of the presence of my dear friend and mentor who left us much too early.

"Welcome everyone," I gushed into the microphone. "Thank you all so much for being here tonight. If you're wondering why you're here, it's because you were in Shepard's shoebox."

A stunned chuckle broke out. I held up the cardboard box and shared the story of the index cards and the condolences. I spoke of Boycie's legacy and the miracle of the new school, which bears her name. I shared stories of Boycie's prodding and her declaration that she would raise the funding. I talked about our beautiful scholars who slept in shelters and cars and on roadsides. I thanked Shepard and the Ansley family and all who had believed in this dream. At the end of the night, the enthusiasm for this groundbreaking program was evident on the faces of all who attended. It was a beautiful celebration of an incredible woman and a bold new program to care for the children in our community.

As I sat with my husband at our favorite pizza place on that cool fall night in 2018, relishing the success of the endeavor, I was proud and humbled. I was tired and absolutely overcome with joy. From the moment the spark of an idea had come to me to do something for the children falling through the cracks of the system, I had dreamed deep and kept walking. The road had been challenging, but I was never alone. The Boyce L. Ansley School was a reality. It was making a difference in the world. I had no doubt that it was divinely convened. We had accomplished what so many said couldn't be done, and I loved that school. I loved the young scholars, their families, and our small but mighty staff. I jokingly called the school my fifth child. The work was hard and stressful and completely all-consuming, but I felt as if it were a part of me. Little did I know—as I bathed in the joy and wonder of that evening—that within three years of its opening, the school would continue to grow but without a place for me.

CHAPTER TWO

The Tapestry of Me

*Be who God created you to be,
and you will set the world on fire.*

—ST. CATHERINE OF SIENNA

"Drink this all down, honey, and then stay close to the bathroom," said the nurse.

I was eight years old, and nothing about the tiny cup the kind nurse was handing me looked appealing. Tentatively, I took the first sip. It was thick and oily, and I knew I was going to throw it up before I could get it all down. A shot of Castor oil. Forty-five years later and the thought of it still makes me gag.

I had been admitted to the children's hospital in Birmingham, Alabama, that morning to undergo testing for recurrent and debilitating stomach pain. The wires and the tubes and the castor oil and all the adults whispering and consulting but not ever really saying what was happening were only making my stomach cramp more. I felt like maybe grown-ups had a different idea about what hurt and what was scary because for the next week, every time I heard someone say, "This won't hurt, honey," or "This won't taste too awful," it meant something really bad and scary was about to happen.

For as far back as I can remember, I was plagued with excruciating stomach pains. I was scared to eat, and I was scared not to eat. When my stomach hurt, I was frightened that I would throw up. I hated throwing up. That might have been my biggest fear—paralyzing me more than the actual pain—but the pain was intense. I missed birthday parties and playdates. I spent a lot of time in the nurse's office at school. Finally, my pediatrician suggested that I be admitted to the hospital for testing. SEVEN days. In today's world, you can have open-heart surgery and be out of the hospital in a day. But back then—I was admitted for a full week. I'm still not sure if they thought something was seriously wrong with me or if they were simply out of options. Nonetheless, my mom and I packed up and headed to the children's hospital while my dad and a series of babysitters stayed with my younger sisters.

My room was fine. It was a private room with a bed, bathroom, and a big window. There was a playroom down the hall with all kinds of toys and brightly colored furniture. The best thing was that there was a girl my age right next door. She was nice and funny, and we became friends. We watched television together in her room and played board games. We talked about all the scary testing and how it made us feel. I think she had been there a long time. She didn't have any hair, and I secretly wondered if I might lose my hair, too. We never really talked about why we were there, but her friendship saved me during that long week.

One day near the end of my stay when I returned from a particularly painful and disgusting test (a barium enema—feel free to look it up if you dare), my friend's room was empty.

"Where'd she go?" I asked my mom.

"She was too sick," said my mom, "and she has gone to be with God."

It took a minute for the words to register, but when they did, I was overwhelmed by disbelief and sadness. We never spoke of it again. I assume my mom thought I forgot, but I think I wasn't sure what to ask or how to comprehend. She was the first person I had known to die. I was eight years old and felt like I hadn't even started living yet. To this day, I don't know her diagnosis or anything about her journey.

I assume she had some sort of cancer. She was clearly much sicker than I was, but she comforted me in my time of distress, and I hope I added even a little joy to her short life.

It's beautiful how children can find friendship and connection when so many things remain unspoken. I assume that like me, she didn't have the words to express her deepest fears. My three strongest memories of that time remain the castor oil, the barium enema, and a very brief friendship between two girls who were scared and in need of a friend.

The results of my seven days of testing were all pretty normal. I was diagnosed with what they called back then a "nervous stomach." I was glad not to have anything serious. I was glad that I wouldn't lose my hair, but I missed my new friend terribly, and my stomach still hurt all the time.

I was prescribed a medication to take three times a day and referred to a child psychologist. I took my little white pill religiously through middle school. Years later when my oldest son was suffering from similar stomach pain, I asked his pediatrician if we could prescribe the same medication for him.

"What you took is actually an opioid," he exclaimed. "We don't prescribe that anymore."

Thankfully, my son's prescription was for over-the-counter medication and talk therapy.

I don't remember much about the child psychologist that my mom took me to see. I don't remember what she looked like or what her office looked like or how often I went to see her. What I do remember is that at some point she asked me if I was worried about anything.

"Well, yes," I said.

I remember thinking, "What kind of question is that? Everyone worries."

"Can you share with me?" she asked.

I took a deep, eight-year-old breath, and the litany began:

"I'm worried that I will throw up. I'm worried that my stomach will hurt. I'm worried I'll do bad in school. I'm worried no one will like me, and, most of all, I'm worried about all the children around the world who are starving. They might die, and they need help. Why is no one helping them?"

"I think," she said in a calm and concerned tone, "you have so many worries in your head that they're overflowing into your stomach."

I think that she was absolutely right. To this day, I haven't completely figured out what to do with all the worries and thoughts that overflow into my stomach. It's been a lifelong struggle. I did eventually come to understand my childhood diagnosis by its more clinical name of irritable bowel syndrome, but the trigger remains the same.

Over the years, therapy has taught me a lot. I'm an empath. I carry the emotions of all those around me. This trait can be a gift but also dangerous. Being an empath means that I'm deeply affected by the emotional state of other people. It's a gift to be so sensitive and aware, but it's also very heavy. Every sad thing I encounter embeds in my soul. It affects my health, my sleep, my ability to sustain deep joy.

"But why," I asked my therapist recently during a session, "do I only seem to carry the pain of others but not the joy?"

"I'm curious about what you did with painful things when you were a child," she said.

My childhood was a topic we had covered repeatedly over the course of our time together. I grew up in a beautiful oasis a handful of miles outside of Birmingham, Alabama, known affectionately as "The Tiny Kingdom." It's a resplendent community filled with history and tradition. My family's connection to the community spanned generations. I was never quite sure where the community ended and my family began. All I knew was that there were family expectations that ran deep. I was taught from a young age that "airing our dirty laundry" was impolite.

"People have their own problems," my mom would say. "They don't need to be burdened with our problems, too."

Now, my therapist looked at me expectantly as she sensed my wheels turning and then an awareness dawn on my face.

"Oh," I said. "I guess I just kept them all inside."

"And then what did you do?" she asked.

"I just stored them up and kept going like I was supposed to," I said.

"I'm curious about what you did with the joyful things," she said.

"I don't know," I answered.

"Could it be that the painful things took up too much room?" she asked.

I soaked up and tucked away so much pain from the world that even surrounded by privilege and beauty, I was unable to find much space for joy. I had permission to share joy. So, joy, I surrendered. I saw the expectation to store pain as a responsibility. Doing it well made me feel like a good person. It was a moment of deep revelation for me. I had no idea what to do with this, but I felt a new clarity. At first, I blamed it all on my parents, but that didn't seem fair. My mind wandered back to a distant memory with my childhood therapist.

"I have a Bible verse I want to share with you," I remembered her saying to me one day. "Jesus says, 'I came that they should have life and have it abundantly.' Can you think about what that might mean?"[4]

I hadn't thought about that conversation in such a long time, but I did still find that verse running through my head from time to time. As I replayed the forgotten moment in my mind, I remembered feeling guilty for having fun when

I knew others in the world were hurting. I remembered thinking joy made me weak. At barely eight years old, I was struggling with living joy. I thought this was how things were supposed to be until my childhood therapist rescued me from the abyss with that piece of scripture. I didn't say it aloud, but I remember in that moment thinking that if God wants me to be happy, then it must be OK to be happy. But I had no idea how to do that.

This struggle, apparently, is just part of what makes me me. It doesn't mean I'm doomed to a life of constant sadness. It simply means I'm complex and whole—divinely made but still very human. It's in this tension that we find out who we really are. I can look back on my life and follow the threads of me—the empath, the introvert, the doer. They are at the same time strengths and challenges. I'm attentive and understanding. I connect deeply with people. I get stuff done. These are good things, but I also struggle with how to unwind from the pain and need of the world. These are the threads that weave together to create the complex person I am. We all have them—those underlying ways of being that are so deeply engrained in our hearts and souls that we assume it's "regular" or "just what everyone else has." The truth is that our threads are uniquely ours. The threads of each of us knot and intertwine in intricate and unique patterns that make every one of us a beautiful and original tapestry of God. The super smart and super intellectual people might call this string theory. I simply call it the woven tapestry of me.

I'm still plagued with stomach issues from time to time, but after more than fifty years of trying and failing, I am finally coming to claim who I am and how I live in the world. Coming to terms with the holy uniqueness and center of me has given me the courage and freedom to live with a little more gusto. My struggles feed into my gifts. It's the sacred dance of life.

When I reflect on my short and tragic friendship with my new friend in the hospital, I realize that my adult self could learn a little from my child self. It was easier back then because we were young, I didn't have the wisdom to understand how sick she was or the words to talk about it. We were just two young girls finding small doses of connection and joy in a bleak situation. Not only did I not absorb her pain, but I also allowed myself to laugh and play. We let our joy supplant our pain, if only for a moment. I hope I offered her as much comfort and distraction as she offered me.

CHAPTER THREE
A Mother's Love

Hope begins in the dark, the stubborn hope that
if you just show up and try to do the right thing,
the dawn will come. You wait and watch and
work: you don't give up.

—ANNE LAMOTT

My second son, Crawford, has always marched to his own beat. His holy tapestry is beautifully unique. He is bright and loyal, kind and quirky. He is also saddled with some frustrating learning differences. Along with attention deficit disorder and anxiety, he struggles with an extreme form of executive function disorder. He is frequently forgetful, late, disorganized, and disheveled. He knows he is smart. He knows he should be able to handle the activities of daily living in a normal way, but the steps from one task to another always hijack his progress. He is frustrated with himself too much of the time. I am frustrated with (and for) him too much of the time.

As someone who is typically organized and reliable, I have taken it upon myself to fix things for him. When he was little, I spent many, many hours setting up organizational charts with stickers and treats and consequences, but nothing seemed to help. I still find myself getting angry with him for not trying. It seems that it should be so easy for him to focus and get organized. All the chaos makes him even more anxious and probably exacerbates the entire issue. It breaks my heart to watch my son struggle, and much of the time, I feel powerless to do anything to help him. I feel I have failed as a parent. We both feel helpless.

When he was in the seventh grade, his school held a parent orientation on a Sunday afternoon from 2–5 p.m. Parents were invited to come to the school and walk through their own child's schedule. His school was a thirty-minute drive from our house. I left forty-five minutes early to ensure that I had plenty of time to park and find my way to the first class. Now, I can't explain what happened or where the time went, but when I was about halfway there, I looked at the clock and realized that I was going to be late. Immediately, my stress level went up. I hate to be late. How could this be happening? I had left with plenty of time.

I arrived at the school at exactly 2 p.m. and whipped into the parking lot. FULL. I tried two different lots. FULL. FULL. The minutes were ticking by faster and faster. I finally pulled alongside the curb in the neighborhood surrounding the school. I rushed into the building to find that I had actually missed nothing more than the initial social time. Tragedy averted.

I grabbed Crawford's schedule and headed to reading. All went well in the class. I took copious notes, surveyed the classroom, got a sense of the teacher, and headed upstairs to math. As the class was about to begin, I noticed that I had actually read the schedule incorrectly. U.S. history was first period, reading was second period, and math not until third. How had this happened? Flushed and embarrassed, I announced that I had made a mistake and ran downstairs to try and work in a period of U.S. history to get myself back on track. I burst into the room late only to realize that this teacher didn't teach U.S. history this period. I was completely mortified. My heart was racing. My palms were sweating, and I could feel the all-too-familiar red splotches beginning to creep up my neck. The fear of losing control was consuming me. I left the class and just stood in the hall trying to collect my breath.

The bell rang for second period to end, and I headed back to the math room, trying not to make too much eye contact with the teacher. I had missed U.S. history, but at least I was back on schedule. What must these people think of me?

Fourth period was art. It was across the courtyard in another building. It was a long way to go in a short time. I entered chatting with another parent and immediately felt eyes upon us. The teacher was staring directly at me—his glare piercing me.

"This is what I do to my students who talk in my class. Stare them down," he said.

The building stress of not being in control, of making a bad impression, was nipping at my heels. I could hardly breathe. As I sat trying to listen and collect my breath, the principal interrupted over the PA system. There were some cars parked along the curb in the surrounding neighborhood that were in jeopardy of being ticketed or towed. Could one of those be my car? Most definitely. My panic grew exponentially. Could this day get any worse? I couldn't leave this class mid-lecture. I can only imagine how this teacher would react to that. If I waited until the class was over to move my car, I would miss science—my son's most challenging class. I opted to leave the car. Ticket, towing, I would just have to deal with that later. When the bell rang, I ran back across the courtyard to science with no incident, but I was so preoccupied with the state of my car that I hardly heard a word the teacher said in his presentation.

After science, I made the decision to skip P.E. and try to find the U.S. history teacher. He was alone in his classroom, and after I bumbled and stumbled through my reason for missing his class, he gave me all the details I had missed. Thank goodness for an understanding teacher.

I left the school and walked tentatively to my car (which was still there and un-ticketed) to begin my trip home. As I drove away from the school still feeling stressed and confused as to how all this could have happened, I realized that this is how my son feels each and every day. I know he tries. I know he cares. I know he is anxious and embarrassed each time he forgets or runs late. I have no idea how my day got so sideways. It wasn't like me to not be in control and in line. I count it as a divine glimpse into understanding because after this experience, I was able to see Crawford's struggles through different eyes.

My other boys and my daughter have their own issues and quirks, but they've figured out how to "be" in the world. They figured out how to "do" school. Their social skills came relatively easily. They could take on the daily tasks of living without too much guidance, but Crawford has travelled a more complicated road. I've always told him that he puts his beautiful "Crawford spin" on everything he does and while that makes life so much richer and more interesting, it also makes everything more difficult.

Crawford is literally a genius, but he has always struggled with social cues and attention skills. He would be in the bathroom for an hour (supposedly brushing his teeth as we all waited impatiently at the door) and would emerge with dramatic and detailed stories about aliens and armies and adventures. His teeth remained unbrushed.

"Crawford, did you brush your teeth?" I would ask.

"What? Um, I think," he would respond.

"Crawford, the sink is dry, and the toothbrush and toothpaste are in the cabinet."

"Oh. I guess I forgot."

His intellect has always been as robust as his energy and imagination. He could read when he entered kindergarten, but he struggled to sit in the circle or follow directions or listen before speaking. He struggled to make friends. The rule at their school was that if a child went an entire week without breaking a class rule, Friday held a trip to the prize basket with all the trinkets and whatnots and tiny plastic toys a child could want. By lunchtime each Monday, Crawford's hopes of a Friday prize-basket visit had already been dashed.

It took him the entire math block in school to begin focusing on math. By the time his brain was ready for math, math was over. The class had moved on. He was always a few steps behind, but he was so smart. He didn't really need the instruction, so he just imagined and joked and wrestled with his desk mates. The best teachers (of which he had many) understood what was happening and worked with us to accommodate Crawford, but he spent many days in the time-out corner at school. Recently, Crawford reflected that he didn't even realize the time-out corner was a punishment.

"I loved not having to participate and interact. I loved just sitting alone, daydreaming with my imaginary friends," he confessed. "The teachers thought they were punishing me, but they were really just sending me to my happy place."

Crawford's issues began to catch up with him in the third grade. He would emerge from school at the end of each day with a hole chewed in the front collar of his shirt. His hair was disheveled. His backpack was unzipped, and papers sputtered to the ground in his wake. It was like watching the Pig Pen character from the Peanuts cartoon who was permanently surrounded by a cloud of dust and confusion.

Our home life was suffering, as well. Homework and basic activities of daily living required all-hands-on-deck. Our entire family was feeling the stress, and my beautiful, smiling, funny boy was slipping deeper and deeper into an imaginary world where he knew how to fit in.

I will be forever grateful to his insightful third-grade teacher who admitted to me that she believed his current school couldn't serve him well. She offered to help me research alternative programs. Her honesty and true love of my incredible, complicated child was a gift, but the decision to pull Crawford from the sweet, Catholic school in our neighborhood was soul-bending. We loved that school. The school loved our children. They were like part of our family. My conversation with the principal to discuss our decision to move Crawford only further proved the quality of community we were giving up. The principal could not have been more supportive.

"I believe you're doing the right thing," she said, "but please know that there's always room here for him, and we'll always do everything we can to support his journey."

After a significant amount of research and testing, we decided to enroll Crawford in a private school that had a program for neurodivergent children. It was expensive and far away, but the program was top-notch. As miserable as he was, Crawford didn't want to move to a new school. He hated school—any school. One morning in January, we dropped his siblings at school and told him we were going on a field trip. We made the long drive (nearly an hour in morning traffic) to what we hoped would be his new school. As soon as Crawford realized what was happening, his backseat chatter and excitement ceased. He became quiet and teary and didn't want to get out of the car. The director of admissions met us, greeting us with a handshake and for Crawford, a can of Coke and an invitation to tour the school on a golf cart. The deal was done. Crawford had found his home.

His teachers were absolutely incredible. They were skilled in supporting students with Crawford's differences. He blossomed. Years later, when I spoke with a mom who reached out because she was having similar issues with her son, I commented that the move to this program had saved our family. She told me later that at that time she didn't understand what I was saying, but after enrolling her son, she saw firsthand the calm and healing that support for her son had given her entire family. We didn't even realize the stress we were under until Crawford began to progress through the specialized program.

Even with all the expense and expertise, Crawford still needed an advocate to keep him from slipping through the cracks. It took an entire team of people dedicated to Crawford's success to usher him through school. Even with his off-the-charts IQ and his team of experts at his side, the journey was still complicated. We were so privileged to have the resources and the network to guide our son, but I still found myself spending a lot of time fighting for his rights.

I remember when he was a junior in high school and a teacher asked me why Crawford didn't have the accommodation that allowed him to circle the answer on a standardized test rather than fill in the bubbles on the worksheet. I didn't even know that was an option.

"Oh yes," the administrator said when I inquired about this accommodation. "His testing indicates visual processing disorder. He definitely fits the criteria."

"Why doesn't he have it?" I asked.

"No one ever requested it. If you want me to add it, we can begin allowing him this accommodation now," she explained.

For seven years he had been in this program surrounded by a team of experts and somehow this had never come up. When a child is struggling with multiple diagnoses, every day is a new mountain to climb. All I wanted was for my son to feel successful and have confidence in himself, but I didn't even know the questions to ask or the systems that existed. Supporting Crawford through school felt like a constant game of Whac-A-Mole. Just as we took care of one pop-up issue, another arose in its place, and the toll it took on Crawford and our whole family was deep and real.

One day, I was on a call with the head of the program. We were having a regular progress check-in, and I began to cry. It was all so hard. Every day was something new. Once my tears began, it was impossible to stop them.

"I'm so sorry," I sobbed through the phone. "I don't know why I'm crying."

We hadn't been discussing anything critical or controversial. My gathering worries had just spilled out into my tear ducts rather than into my stomach. I will never forget the director's response:

"If a mother doesn't cry for her child's pain, who will?"

Being a mom has been one of the greatest joys of my life. Being a mom has also been one of the greatest challenges of my life. I have been so fortunate to have the time and resources and networks to support me in raising my children. I believe most moms want nothing less for their children. How lonely and frustrating and overwhelming it must be for so many women shouldering the vocation of motherhood without enough support. And what about the children—innocent and hopeful and counting on the adults in the world to protect them and teach them?

CHAPTER FOUR
A Mother's Struggle

*To pay attention, this is our endless
and proper work.*

It was spring 2015. A month had passed since my initial conversation with Boycie about the need for a school for children without housing. The seed that had been planted during that short exchange still rumbled in my head but seemed an impossible dream. On this day, I was heading to a meeting at Crossroads, the homeless-serving agency where I regularly volunteered. As the story goes, Crossroads began in 1974 when a member of St. Luke's Episcopal Church handed a homeless man a sandwich. Today, Crossroads is a refuge for people who are experiencing homelessness in Atlanta.

I live on a tree-lined street in a quaint neighborhood just east of downtown Atlanta. I frequently made the fifteen-minute drive from my neighborhood to Crossroads. St. Luke's is my family's church, and Crossroads will always be one of our favorite organizations. The entire St. Luke's campus is like a second home to me. I was so familiar with the well-worn path of the route from home to church that I had become numb to the stark shift in landscape between my neighborhood and the Courtland Street corridor where the campus of St. Luke's and Crossroads hold a prominent place. Crime, homelessness, and economic blight are in full display on almost every corner. People sleep on the sidewalks. People with no place to go wander through traffic. Fights break out. The area is a food desert, and absolutely no place for a child to spend the day. Yet I (along with most Atlanta in-town dwellers) drive this path so often that we sadly become somewhat immune to the scene.

But this day, something was different. On this day, I noticed. From the comfort of my car, I noticed a woman sitting on the curb of the busy four-lane road. I had to change lanes to avoid passing too close to her. She had her head in her hands, a cart of belongings beside her, and four small children running around her feet. One of the children had no shirt and two had no shoes. The children were much younger than my children, and in that moment, I felt that mother's pain. I felt her agony and worry and distress. I didn't know her or anything about her situation, but I saw her hopelessness, and it floored me. I had four children and knew how even with all my safety nets and privileges, I often felt overwhelmed and exhausted. And then the question hit me like a punch in the gut. What if one of her children is struggling like my Crawford? I had shed more tears and lost more sleep over my sweet, brilliant boy than I can ever measure, but I never doubted that we would have a roof over our heads, food on the table, money to pay for any help he needed, and a loving family and community to support us even when it seemed like our whole world might be falling apart.

I was only one block from the St. Luke's/Crossroads campus, and as I pulled into a parking space, I couldn't get the image of that mother out of my mind. Something had to be done to help her. How many more mothers were out there in the same situation? I took my place at the scheduled meeting, but I couldn't focus on the agenda. The image of those children and that overwhelmed woman collided with the pain and frustration I felt in navigating the world with my son. The heaviness of the situation settled in my heart. I couldn't just let it go. I was accustomed to carrying around the weight of pain in the world, but something about this felt different. Mixed with the agony of the situation, I felt a strange sense of hope.

After my committee meeting ended, I asked the executive director, a compassionate and experienced professional, if he had a moment to talk. He cared for people who were suffering and invisible every day. I wanted his guidance on what I could do to be part of the solution. We sat in his tiny office which looked out onto the same street where I encountered the mother. On any given day, there is a steady stream of people going up and down the street and coming in and out of the building looking for someone—anyone—to help. They want to be seen and heard. They long to find a friend to walk beside them as they find stability and healing.

"What is the landscape of the childcare opportunities for mothers without resources?" I asked.

"It's complicated," he said.

He went on to explain the details of federal and state assistance, sliding fee scales, and income verification. When he finished, I was almost more confused than when we began the conversation.

"So, what if I can start a fund to supplement the cost of childcare for these families?" I asked. "Could that help them find long-term quality care?"

Unfortunately, I learned that once these parents begin receiving any private financial support, they quickly become ineligible for many of the public programs. The last thing I wanted was for my ignorance to create another roadblock.

In his book, *Toxic Charity*, Robert Lupton laments that all too often, well-meaning people decide the "best" way to help without truly taking time to understand the people they are serving or the problem they are addressing.[5]

Then a wild idea came to me.

"So why can't we start a campaign to raise money to create our own private childcare program?"

Even as I said it, I wanted to laugh at the absurdity of my own idea, but the executive director's face lit up.

"That's an amazing idea. Let's do it! Can we open next month?"

At this, I did laugh.

"No. I'm serious. Could we open in the fall?" he asked with great enthusiasm.

Could we put this thing together in six months? Could we put this together at all?

"Let me do some thinking, and we can reconnect next week," I said.

St. Luke's Episcopal Church is a large downtown parish with a history of incubating and spinning off innovative nonprofit organizations in the city. Although St. Luke's is located in downtown Atlanta, most members drive from other neighborhoods to attend. A few years earlier, the church had completed a large capital campaign and renovated the children's wing. The space was absolutely beautiful. During the grand-opening tour, a church member commented that the space was so nice that we might even want to consider starting a preschool for church members who work downtown.

"It would provide a service to the members as well as some income for the church," suggested the woman.

"If this church is ever going to start any preschool, it will be to serve those who live in our neighborhood," the priest exclaimed with great intention and authority.

For some reason, those words of his from years ago had lodged in my brain, and now, with this new notion rising in my soul, I decided we should have a conversation.

We sat in the study attached to his office. The room was comfortable and bright. From the window, the church playground and the roof of the building that housed Crossroads were visible.

"I have a harebrained idea," I said to him, but as I began to explain, he began to nod and smile.

He immediately offered one of the children's Sunday School rooms to house the program.

It's so amazing how God just puts situations in your path and as you timidly step forward, doors begin to open.

I was nervous and exhilarated and hopeful, and I was going to need some help.

I recruited a small but mighty group of women from different areas of my life to sit and brainstorm with me. Each brought a unique set of skills and experiences. We met in the midtown condo of one of our new committee members. Over plates of chicken salad and fruit, we dreamed. After much debate and discussion, we decided to begin our journey with a one-morning-per-week parents' morning-out program. It would be available Tuesdays from 9 a.m. to 1 p.m. Crossroads would refer children of their guests. When Crossroads parents had a job interview or other appointments, Crossroads Kids, as we named it, would take care of their children for four hours. All they had to do was register with the caseworker at Crossroads. Because Crossroads ran a meal program, they offered to provide a hot breakfast and a sack lunch to each child registered in the program.

We hired the director of the church nursery, who had a degree in education, to run the program. Her pay for four hours of work per week was funded by a couple of donations. We recruited a team of volunteers who committed to being with her in the classroom one Tuesday per month. And we were off.

Between September and Christmas break 2015, we had between five and twelve children each Tuesday. Some only came once or twice, but there were others who came every week. They ate two meals, participated in specially designed activities to build social skills and pre-reading skills, and their parents had a moment to take care of life without children in tow. I knew this wasn't solving the bigger problem of educational inequity, but I was glad to be doing something to help in the smallest way.

Overall, the program was running smoothly. Both participants and volunteers were excited, but before long, a disturbing trend began to emerge. We had a number of elementary-school-aged children who came to the program. One twelve-year-old girl came with her brother and sister almost every Tuesday. Why wasn't she in school? We had assumed that money was the issue for lack of early childcare, and that once public school was possible, all children were served. Now, I began to question my own assumptions. Was this program actually helping? Was there something more we needed to do? How were these children supposed to thrive without an education? And always, in the back of my mind, what about the children who have learning differences like my son? How would they ever survive?

Then, one cold day in December, we encountered our first crisis.

Parents completed paperwork for the program with their case manager at Crossroads. The forms included all the details you would put on any enrollment questionnaire.

So, when a little girl fell ill during program hours, we pulled her file and called her mother—whose cell phone had been disconnected. We then called the shelter of residence listed (Crossroads provides services but no shelter), and because the shelter didn't have written permission to give us any information, they wouldn't even confirm if the mother and children were residents.

"Look," I said in frustration, "if the mother does live there, could you please get her a message to call me ASAP? Otherwise, I'm going to need to call an ambulance to take the child to the nearest hospital."

It was becoming clear that we were in over our heads. Fortunately the mom called back and was able to get the child to an urgent care facility, where she was treated for a childhood virus and released. But the incident raised so many new questions of liability.

Our small organizing group met over Christmas break for some serious discussions. What were we doing? What was our goal? Were we on the right path? Even though we had more questions than answers, one thing was clear: We needed to pivot. So, we made the difficult decision to suspend our program and regroup.

CHAPTER FIVE
Pivot

Sometimes good things fall apart so better things could fall together.

—MARILYN MONROE

The decision to suspend Crossroads Kids was difficult. We weren't sure what the next step should be. We knew this wasn't the end of the journey. I think I already knew deep down what we needed to do, but it took me some encouragement to get to that point. My friend and mentor, Boycie, came hurtling into my thoughts. She agreed with the need for new educational opportunities for children without housing, and most of all, she believed in my ability to make a program happen.

The only experience I had with education was from my own time in school—where I had studied journalism and theology—and from my role as a parent guiding my four children through school. I wasn't equipped to create an actual school. Crossroads Kids had proven to be more complicated than any of us imagined, and it was only a baby step into the bigger issue. There was no good reason I should think I could do something that no expert professional educator had done, yet I couldn't talk myself out of it. It felt like a spark in my soul that wouldn't be contained. And so, with great trepidation and great excitement, I was finally able to tell Boycie that I was on the path. I promised her I would begin some feasibility studies in the community just to see what the options might be. I still mourn the fact that she never saw the outcome of her encouragement.

In the spring of 2016, I regathered our small planning group to begin doing some research. We began by talking with homeless-serving agencies and many of the families they served. We wanted to really understand the logistics and the challenges. We wanted to know the history of the families and their experiences in the educational system. We wanted to know what the caseworkers perceived as important or lacking. We wanted to understand as much as we could about why so many children without stable housing were falling through the cracks of the educational system. We wanted our next step to be something that could fit into the landscape of existing programs and schools and fill a gap. We wanted to be certain that we were filling a true need in a way that was impactful, deep, and lasting. To do this, we needed to understand. This was one of the weaknesses of our first program. We were too excited and began too quickly. We didn't do quite enough research. I had fallen into the exact model of blind charity that I so vocally oppose. Our program didn't truly offer a solution, only another band-aid.

As it turns out, only two blocks from the church campus (on the campus of another church) there is an established daycare program for children living in area shelters. Our group arranged a tour with the executive director.

The day of our tour, a driving rain fell in the city. Water rushed up and over the downtown sidewalks, and the wind blew steadily down the street. Since parking was scarce, walking the two blocks made the most sense even in the stormy conditions. As we trudged up the sidewalk with umbrellas pressing against the wind and rain jackets zipped up to our chins, I couldn't help but think of the mom I had seen sitting on this very curb just over one year ago. Where was she on this day? The streets were quiet except for a few people ducking beneath overhangs. It was miserable to be outside. What if you had no other choice?

We arrived at the center ten minutes later, dripping and sloshing in our wet jackets and shoes. The executive director greeted us warmly, and after we hung up our rain-soaked outer layers, she began showing us through the center. Their program was incredible—much like what we had hoped our first program would become. The organization served families with children between six months and four years. They had beautiful classrooms, energetic and caring teachers, onsite medical, dental, and mental health professionals for the children, as well as case management and job training for the parents.

"What an incredible program you all have built," I said after our tour.

"We're so proud of our work," said the executive director. "We wish we could serve every child that needs us."

Space and funding were their barriers. They also shared with us that it was sometimes difficult to successfully transition these children—whose families lacked stable and permanent housing—into a public school experience that could serve them upon completing their program. We wanted to find out why.

The week following our initial tour, we were invited to return to the organization for a conversation with some of the past and present parents of children in the program. I was so moved by the honesty and vulnerability of these parents. One by one, they shared their hopes and dreams for their children, their frustrations and struggles with their situations, their own memories of their time in school, and their personal and family goals. It was an honor to be in the company of mothers and fathers who, just like me, wanted nothing more than the very best for their children. This program was a gift, but they were all concerned about the next stage. Those with older children shared their struggles.

Annie and John had two young girls. They worked full-time. One worked the day shift and the other the night shift. Their combined income didn't cover housing, so they lived in a family shelter. At 3 a.m. each day, Annie would wake the young girls and load them onto the city bus that was bound for the subway station. This is where John met them after his shift. Annie took the subway to her job, and John wandered the streets with the girls until it was time to take them to school. (In most cases, once you leave a shelter in the morning, you aren't allowed to return until the evening.) Both girls were tired and hungry. Both girls frequently complained of stomach pain and fell asleep in class. The older sister was so weak and unbalanced that the teachers suspected she might have an undiagnosed medical problem, but they were unsure how to proceed with testing. The girls were offered time to sleep in class, yet their learning suffered. The family was stressed and frustrated.

Latisha was a single mother of two young boys. She took shift work when she could find it but couldn't afford stable housing. As is common, Latisha and her boys moved regularly from short-term shelters to friends' couches to motels. Each time they moved, her nine-year-old son had to change elementary schools. Although there is a federal mandate for public schools to transport children without stable housing back to their school of origin, we learned that this is usually a logistical impossibility. In most cases, the school system was willing to provide transportation for her older son back to his school of origin, but due to bus routes, her son would have to be picked up each morning at 4:30 a.m. and wouldn't be dropped off until after 6 p.m. There was simply no other way to make it work. So, while the younger son remained stable in this private daycare, the older boy changed schools every few months. Research shows that each time a child changes schools, the child loses up to three months of reading and math learning.[6] With every move, her older son fell further and further behind.

Too often, the perception of people who lack stable housing is that they're not smart or don't care, but the courage, love, and fortitude of these parents overwhelmed me. They weren't satisfied with their current situations. They knew what they wanted. They knew what their children needed to succeed, and they were doing everything in their power to make their dreams a reality. One mother told me that simply the opportunity to be heard and seen and to be offered some amount of agency in the next steps was a gift she would always cherish.

After our parent groups, we continued our community conversations and research by meeting with public school administrators and potential funders. Every education professional we met expressed a genuine concern for their ability to adequately serve students without stable housing. Children experiencing homelessness struggle with inadequate sleep and nutrition. Many also deal with significant trauma and low social-emotional skills. The teachers simply can't always serve the very specific needs that unstable housing brings.

And there it was again—that seemingly impossible call to start a school. I had tried to ignore it, but it wouldn't leave me alone. From the beginning, I had dreamed of a program as highly esteemed and successful as the program my son attended, but one that was financially supported by the community rather than the families. Didn't these children and their families deserve the same opportunities as my children and family?

Bolstered by our research and the obvious need for a new way to support these children and their families, I scheduled meetings with several large foundations and community leaders. I wasn't asking for money, I simply wanted to make sure we had the buy-in of the community at-large. I was confident that the information we had gathered would create a successful pitch for financial and civic support. I was wrong.

I went into my first meeting with the confidence of a tree with deep roots. I was meeting with a woman who was both a veteran community organizer and a city government official. We sat in a large meeting space at St. Luke's. Empty tables scattered the room. I sat with a colleague and our guest. The three of us seemed small in the large and mostly empty room. I welcomed her and began explaining our journey, our research, and our plans. I had charts and graphs and proposals to back up my information.

She took a long look at everything and then said, "And who are you? What do you do?"

I stammered and faltered and sheepishly replied, "I'm just a concerned citizen."

"Well, that's very nice," she said, "but I think you're in over your head."

If she had reached out and patted me on the head, it would not have been more humiliating. For almost twenty years, I had stayed home with my children and struggled with my purpose and worth. I loved my children, and I loved that I had the opportunity to stay home with them. I wouldn't have changed that for the world, but I also struggled with the cultural message that I wasn't smart enough or skilled enough or energetic enough to make it in the professional world. Her comment wrapped all my insecurities into one tiny package and laid them bare on the table.

Thank goodness my colleague and friend was there to close out the meeting and escort our guest to the door because I was absolutely dumbstruck.

"Well," my friend said as she returned to the room alone, "I think we need to come up with a better title for you."

No title seemed appropriate for me. I think I was suffering from a bit of imposter syndrome—seeing all potential titles as too grand or important for my skill and experience. After all, I kept telling myself, I really had no idea what I was doing. And so, I entered my next meeting without a clever idea of what I would say if asked who I was or what I did. Fortunately (and unfortunately), we didn't get that far.

For this meeting, I was the visitor. I arrived at the large downtown building with plenty of time to spare. My husband had once worked in this building, so I knew from experience that our large car would only fit in the parking spaces on the roof of the deck. Up and up and around and around I went as I practiced my speech again and again.

"Hi." I imagined myself saying. "My name is Kate, and I'm a community advocate."

No. That wasn't right.

"Hi," I tried again. "My name is Kate, and I'm a dreamer."

No. That definitely wasn't right.

Two elevator banks and one very long escalator ride later, I was still rolling through titles in my head as I arrived at the entrance to the office. I was escorted to the head of an expansive table in a grand conference room of the large foundation. The executive director and her leadership team listened intently to my plan. Since I hadn't come up with a suitable title for myself, I just launched into the research.

When I finished my presentation, which I thought went well, the executive director looked at me and said, "This will never work. It's a waste of time and resources to try. The focus should be on supporting the public schools rather than competing with them."

Hadn't I just reported that all the public school administrators I'd interviewed agreed with the need for a new type of program? Did she not hear me say that the public schools wanted to partner with us in referring students back and forth?

Just as I was about to speak, one of the other women at the table said, "Yes. I think we all would agree that a program such as this would be a waste of time and money. We stand in support of our public schools."

They didn't care about my title or my credentials. They just thought the whole thing was a bad idea. I thanked them for their time and left yet another meeting completely bewildered.

Meeting after meeting seemed to go the same way. Those who worked in the school system and the families that were struggling all expressed great enthusiasm for our program. Leaders and funders in our community weren't interested.

I've always been a little stubborn, and so after licking my wounds and picking up my pride, I continued the journey.

When I don't know what to do next, Google seems to be my go-to. So, I began Googling to see if there were *any* similar programs in the country. I couldn't find anything exactly like what we envisioned, but there were two programs that piqued my interest—an Episcopal school in Boston and a private school in Oklahoma City. Clearly, my idea wasn't completely off-base.

The heads of the two schools could not have been more kind and helpful. In fact, I was so intrigued that our small committee decided to travel to both schools for in-person visits. After all, I had promised Boycie that I would build a program. More importantly, the families I'd met along the way had become part of me. I couldn't abandon the dream— not just yet.

CHAPTER SIX

Stuck at Home

*What we hunger for perhaps more than
anything else is to be known in our full
humanness, and yet that is often just what we
also fear more than anything else.*

–FREDERICK BUECHNER

The morning of our trip to Boston, my son, Crawford, fell into crisis. In addition to learning differences, Crawford struggled with intense migraine headaches. He often spent time resting in the nurse's office at school or had to miss school altogether. The pain was debilitating and was usually accompanied by vomiting and loss of vision. For a while, his migraines had seemed to calm, but I had noticed a rise in occurrence over the last few months. The day before our trip, Crawford was home from school with another headache. It was one thing to miss a few days in elementary school, but now that he was in high school, it was much harder to keep up. I sat down at my computer to email his teachers about his absence. Almost the exact moment I hit send, a reply came back:

> Crawford has fallen behind in my class. I know he's been dealing with a lot of headaches, but even when he's here, he isn't participating or turning in his work.

I was stunned. I, too, had become concerned about the number of days he had missed over the last months, but he assured me he was working it out with his teachers. Before I could even respond to the message, another reply dinged into my inbox:

> I hope Crawford is feeling better. I've been concerned about his performance in my class lately. His grade has dropped significantly over the past few weeks, and he seems more anxious and scattered than usual.

A panic began to stir in my gut. Crawford's team had set up multiple systems of support for him at school. One of the goals of the system was to keep the parents from having to be the enforcers. It had been scary but also freeing to not be the ones who were constantly checking his grades and assignments and questioning him about his work. The system was designed to allow space for our relationship with Crawford to be more focused on family time and enjoying Crawford's incredible sense of humor, kind heart, and deep thoughts.

We trusted the system. Crawford's dad and I had let go of some of the day-to-day upkeep of Crawford's schooling. His team at school was keeping an eye on him, and now they were alerting us to a growing concern. My stress level continued to rise.

"What?" I thought to myself. "How can this be?"

I should have waited until Crawford was feeling better. I should have taken a deep breath and scheduled some conversations with his team at school. I should have done a lot of things—except what I did.

Crawford was curled up in his bed with the covers completely over his head. I sat on the edge of the bed and placed my hand on his shoulder.

"Crawford?" I said in a voice much calmer than I felt. "Is something going on at school that you want to talk about?"

A groan and a shrug of my hand off his shoulder was his only response.

"Crawford?" I repeated. "I just received emails from your Mandarin teacher and your math teacher that you're falling behind and not turning in your work."

This time, an annoyed voice rose from under the covers.

"Mom, my head really hurts. Everything's fine. I just want to sleep."

Trying to have this conversation at that moment was a mistake. At this point, I should have just left and scheduled that meeting with his team. I should have, but I'm stubborn, and I was worried and stressed. I can fix anything. I could fix this. It was my job as a mother to make sure my children succeeded, and I was clearly failing.

The storm in my head grew. The worry overwhelmed me, and in my usual way, my immediate response was to react rather than to step back and reflect first. I'm not proud of this, but it's my default.

"Crawford," I stubbornly continued. "Everything's not fine. Tell me why you're not turning in your work?"

"Mom, I don't want to talk about it. It's fine," he mumbled from under the covers.

"Crawford," I repeated as I pulled the covers from over his eyes. "I really think your migraines are related to stress. Lately, you've been having so many. Let's figure this out now and your head will feel better."

"NO, Mom. It's fine," he argued, pulling the covers back over his head.

We went back and forth like this for a long time with Crawford getting more upset and agitated and me getting angrier and more desperate. The tears that Crawford began to shed only increased the pain in his head and the anxiety level in the room. No matter what was going on, we could fix this, I thought. We could make a plan and find a way. My sense of urgency grew with every round of prodding and denial, and Crawford's despair and anxiety became a dark cloud that surrounded us both.

I reached out to my school planning committee and told them that I wouldn't be able to accompany them to Boston. My son was struggling, and I needed to be with him.

The next morning, instead of boarding the plane for Boston, I began round fifteen with my son. Our exchange continued much as it had the day before until finally, late in the afternoon, the truth came out in a moment of desperation and exhaustion.

"I can't get my locker open," Crawford shouted.

I think he was as surprised as I was that it had come out of his mouth.

"What?" I asked. "I don't understand."

"My locker," Crawford said. "It's stuck. I can't get it open."

"For how long?" I asked.

"Since the first week of school."

It was almost November.

"You haven't been able to open your locker for three months?"

He nodded, both embarrassed and frustrated that the issue was out.

Slowly the realization dawned on me. He hadn't been able to access his textbooks or notebooks for the entire semester. No wonder he couldn't complete his assignments or participate in class.

"Why didn't you say anything sooner?"

He shrugged.

Some of the trademarks of executive function disorder are the inability to make a game plan and to understand or connect consequences to actions. For Crawford, these deficits were paired with a genius IQ and a highly developed imagination. When the real world was too overwhelming or anxiety-provoking, Crawford had a safe world in his mind where he could happily be. As he was getting older, though, the problems of real life in the real world weren't going away. The consequences (and the headaches—although Crawford and I still disagree on their connection) were growing more complicated and serious.

For the past three months, Crawford hadn't been able to access any of his textbooks. His brain simply couldn't process what to do. To get help, he would have to tell someone that he couldn't figure out how to open his locker.

In his mind, the embarrassment of admitting that was too great to endure. He was already seen by many students as an odd kid. He had dealt with bullying and exclusion for his entire life. When you're in high school, marching to your own drummer isn't an asset. Between his tics and collar chewing, his ill-preparedness and love of his imaginary world, Crawford suffered socially. To admit that he couldn't remember how to open his locker for three months was too embarrassing. So, he just ignored it, and now, everything was starting to crumble.

I should have been more sympathetic. I should have taken him into my arms and hugged him. I should have done a lot of things, but I was so frustrated. I am the queen of executive functioning skills. A good game plan and check list can solve so many problems. Why didn't Crawford just come to me? We could have fixed this. I was angry and frustrated. Why did it take us two full days to get to the bottom of this? I wish I'd taken more time to reflect. I wish I hadn't reacted so quickly, but that was my issue. It was years later that Crawford confessed to me that my need to fix every problem he presented only increased his stress.

"Sometimes," he told me (years later when he had found the words and self-awareness), "I just want you to sit with me for a minute and let me feel the stress and your love before we jump into fix-it mode because that mode makes me so anxious."

But on that day, we weren't there yet, and my drive to fix was strong. I put in a call to the school office. The assistant principal answered the phone.

"My son is unable to open his locker. Is there someone there who can assist him?" I asked.

"Those lockers are so old. They're constantly getting jammed. Give me his locker number, and I'll meet him there in the morning," he said with no hint of surprise or disdain.

Crawford didn't want to go. He was anxious and embarrassed and ashamed, but he went. The assistant principal—who everyone loved—was right there waiting. He asked Crawford to dial in his combination and then with one quick flick of a metal rod in the corner of the door, the ancient locker swung open.

"Thank you," Crawford said timidly.

"No problem," he responded. "This happens all the time. Let me know if it gets stuck again."

The hole Crawford had dug himself into over the past three months was deep. He would have to work hard to dig himself out. He had late assignments to make up, poor test scores to pull up, and a lot of reading to catch up on.

We still refer to that story as "The Locker Incident." While it might seem like a small thing—to have your locker jammed—my son's ability to navigate the situation was hijacked by his extraordinary mind. Even in a renowned program with advocates and safety nets and every support technique in place, my son almost fell through the cracks. That was why the committee was in Boston. That was why we went to Oklahoma City. That was why we couldn't sit back and do nothing.

CHAPTER SEVEN
A Leap of Faith

Walker, your footsteps are the road,
and nothing more. Walker, there is no road,
the road is made by walking.

—ANTONIO MACHADO

Following our trips, three things were clear to our planning committee.

One: There was no more research to be done.

Two: There was no doubt that we had to do something.

Three: There was no consensus on what that should be.

Our focus groups, meetings, and trips to Oklahoma City and Boston had given us a broad and substantial picture of the issue. Children without housing were falling through the cracks of our educational system in overwhelming numbers.

Should we join forces with the existing early childcare facility for children in shelters, should we create a fund to support the work of our public school system possibly with an after-school program, or should we create an independent private school? Our research showed that even among community leaders, funders, students, and educators, there was no obvious path. It was our job to decide where we were going to stand. No matter which of the paths we chose, there would be naysayers. The only thing we knew for certain was that doing nothing was not an option. We'd already started and stopped once, so this time we wanted to get it right.

In early 2017, I was introduced to a local business coach. She ran a successful business providing strategic planning and career and business development for professionals. I told her about my current journey, and she generously offered to give us four hours of time without charge. I wasn't sure what we could accomplish in four hours, but it was a place to start.

In February of 2017, our small committee of five gathered on the cheery sunporch of the coach's home with laptops and tentative expectations of what our morning would hold. She began by having us list all the iterations of the program that we were considering: a preschool collaboration with the agency down the street, an after-school program with public school partnership, or a privately funded independent school. Even among the committee members, there was no consensus. We each leaned toward a different choice for different reasons. "If the funders aren't on board, there is no way to succeed." "If it isn't helpful to the families, we are wasting everyone's time." "If it's a good program, the money will come." There were positives and negatives for each of our scenarios. We were stuck.

Our business coach (I have to say that I was still in awe that an actual business coach was taking us seriously—impostor syndrome is tough to shake!) led us in a SWOT analysis for each proposed iteration. A SWOT analysis is a tool used in strategic planning which asks participants to make lists of the Strengths, Weaknesses, Opportunities, and Threats for each model.

We spent the next hour naming all the pros and cons we could think of for each option. The words filled the room like popcorn, fast and surprising. Once our minds were fully emptied, we sat back and looked at the lists forming columns on the large computer screen. I'm not sure how our facilitator kept up, but she had been able to record each of our varied descriptors in clear and organized graphics.

She gave us time to study our work and reflect individually and privately. The room was quiet as we all reviewed our thoughts. When I really looked at the lists, the answer was so very clear to me: we needed to go all in and start a full school. That idea terrified me so much that I didn't know if I had the courage, stamina, intelligence, or time to make it happen. The words of the very first community leader resonated in my mind, "You're in way over your head."

After a few minutes of quiet, the business coach gave us each $100 in play money. The game was for each of us to donate some or all of our "funds" to one or more of the proposed models knowing the strengths and weaknesses of each. We took our time—each pondering and analyzing to ourselves. If I were a funder, I knew where my money would go. Without hesitation, I "donated" it all to the full school. It frightened me to the core, but I had to go with my gut.

When the giving was complete, we counted the donations. I must not have been the only one in our group who recognized the bold statement of our complex pro/con list. Much to all our outward surprise and trepidation, our third model, our privately funded independent school, had received an overwhelming majority of the funding. It wasn't even close. We had picked the hard one. We had picked the expensive one. We had picked the most unrealistic one. What were we doing?

The business coach looked at our doubtful faces and began to speak.

"You have done the research. You have analyzed the models. You have made your choice. Trust in this process," she said.

Could we really do this? It did feel right, but it was going to be a difficult endeavor. The families would be happy. The caseworkers would be supportive, but there was that one entry on our analysis that frightened me to no end: "The ladies think this is a bad idea."

"The Ladies" were the many female foundation trustees and executive directors we had met. All of them echoed the same message: "This is a bad idea." Could we overcome this barrier to funding? All we could do was take the next step and see what happened. As we left the security of the sunny porch, I felt the exhilaration—yet the weight—of the journey we had just agreed to make.

I knew a retired gentleman who gave a significant amount of money to the community. He had been an entrepreneur and was a prolific supporter of area nonprofits. He always seemed to give transformational gifts. There's a universal problem with funding. Most funders want to fund organizations that are solid. They often require three to five years of audited financials and a strong list of current supporters in order to make a gift. Very few funders want to make "angel investments"—gifts to innovative start-ups.

Making an angel investment means understanding that your dollars could do something truly transformational or be lost in the land of failed ideas. This gentleman had a history of being first. He did his due diligence. He was a wise business professional, but his entrepreneurial spirit was evident in his giving. I decided the next right step would be to invite him to lunch and share the dream.

During his career, men made the decisions, and women took the notes or stayed home with the children. I knew he'd be more comfortable discussing a financial matter with a man, so I enlisted the help of my husband.

My email invitation read:

> My husband and I would like to invite you to lunch to share a business idea we have.

He accepted, and we settled on a place and a date.

I was so nervous. We had chosen a restaurant that was very familiar to me. It was quiet when we arrived, and we were seated at a booth in the corner of the room. My husband and I sat on one side, leaving the other bench open for our guest. He arrived moments after we did, shook hands with us, and took a seat across the table. He and my husband engaged in some small talk about their business careers and financial matters until the waitress came to take our order.

Once we had ordered, I began my pitch.

"I have an idea that I think might interest you," I said.

"You do?" he said in surprise.

It wasn't a condescending comment. It was more like he was intrigued by the thought. Was he intrigued by the thought of a woman having a business idea or was he simply intrigued by the thought of a new business idea? Either way, he was intrigued and smiling—ready to hear what I had to say.

I made my pitch. I shared research, statistics, and stories. I shared our strategic plan.

"I have a draft of a budget here," I said as I handed over the document. "I estimate that it will cost us $200,000 to open the doors. Would you be willing to fund a third of that amount if my husband and I fund a third and the community funds the final third?"

I could tell the wheels were turning in his head, but less than a few seconds passed before he said, "That rounds up to $67,000. Where should I send the check?"

I was in shock.

"OK," I responded, trying not to smile too broadly. "St. Luke's is acting as our fiscal agent during the start-up, so you can send a check to St. Luke's made out to the church and designated to this program. I can't tell you how grateful I am. Thank you."

"My mother was a teacher," he said. "She used to go around knocking on doors in our community to make sure children were able to get to school. This would make her very happy. Thank you for doing it."

This was a fact I hadn't even known. I was in constant wonder of the way the birth of this project so often seemed to be written in the stars. Time and again, I was overwhelmed by radical amazement and gratitude for the strength, the opportunity, and the uncovering of new and surprising connectedness.

As we finished our lunch, he and my husband returned to their conversation. I listened and nodded and laughed in all the right places, but my mind was spinning. There was no turning back. We were going to build a school. Now, I just had to figure out how to raise $67,000 from the community and build a school.

Over the years and until his death in 2022, our angel investor's belief in the work and his support of the program through both his financial gifts and his network were foundational to the school's early success. He preferred to stay anonymous in his giving, but everyone always knew when he was involved. He was a keen businessman and a bold visionary. When new programs popped up and began making an impact, you could be pretty sure that he had been there from the beginning, but he didn't require the spotlight. He simply wanted to use the fruits of his work to create a bold legacy of good in the world.

Much like my mentor (and his dear friend) Boycie, I knew that if he believed in me, I was on the right track. This was really happening.

CHAPTER EIGHT
All In

A caring teacher had just scooped a little girl into her arms and was carrying her across the playground. The photo showed only the back of the teacher, but the little girl's face was full frame—her smile inviting all to want to know more about who and where she was. It was a stock photo that we found on the internet to don our first piece of school publicity, but it said a thousand words in its placement. In later years, when our materials showed photos of our actual scholars, people would ask about the little girl in the first photo. "How's she doing?" "Is she still a student?" Her face connected with our community in lasting and powerful ways. People were always surprised to hear that her image was free stock footage found online. In that moment, on that day, the little girl from the internet introduced the potential of our big idea.

Our new logo and tagline were also displayed prominently on the flyer and the large screen in the front of the parish hall at St. Luke's. It was a Sunday morning in early fall, and the church had invited all to come and hear about "The Next Big Thing."

We were ready to announce the dream of The Boyce L. Ansley School. We had adopted the tagline "Beyond Circumstance" to announce that the goal of this program would be to support and equip children experiencing homelessness to move beyond their current circumstance and write their own stories of success. Our slide presentation featured vignettes from our research, interviews, and focus groups. It laid out the issue and our belief that this bold and innovative program could begin a movement to end generational poverty in Atlanta.

When the doors opened, I was overwhelmed by the number of people who took a seat in the rows of chairs that filled the parish hall. By the time we began the program, every seat was filled, and the room was packed. One of the priests at St. Luke's was a dear friend of mine and a member of our start-up committee. She had donated funding from her budget for us to create the website that we would unveil today. She stepped to the microphone with a smile on her face and opened the gathering with a prayer.

Then she said, "St. Luke's has a rich history of incubating innovative ministries that grow to become change-making organizations in our community."

She listed several examples including The Atlanta Community Food Bank, The Fraser Center, Midtown Assistance Center, Crossroads, and the Atlanta Center of Self Sufficiency. The list was long and impressive.

"It's been a while," she continued, "since St. Luke's last launched a new program, and the time has come. If we're to remain a beacon in the city of Atlanta, it's imperative that we continue to address the problems in our community in bold ways. The Boyce L. Ansley School is our next big thing."

"Many of you know Kate Kennedy," she continued. "She's been an active leader in our parish for years. She saw a need in the community, and for the past few years, she and her small but mighty team have been working diligently to find a solution. I can't wait for you to hear about their bold idea."

The stage was set, and the microphone was mine.

"Good morning, everyone. I'm so glad you could join us today."

I shared our slide presentation and research. I spoke about the issue and some of the families I had met along the way. Then I opened the floor for questions. The energy in the room was high. The support and buy-in of the crowd were palpable. The questions were supportive, inquisitive, and filled with a sense of hope and excitement. In this room, I didn't have to prove myself. People knew me. These people were my church family. They knew my heart, my drive, and my determination. It wouldn't matter to them if I had a title or not. They trusted me. Ironically, this time, unlike in meetings past, I actually did have a title. The last slide of the presentation announced the address of the new website and my name with the word "Founder" underneath.

It's so interesting to me that once I added this title to my name, the level of respect that I received in professional meetings increased dramatically. I hadn't even started anything yet, but somehow, when people saw a business card or a LinkedIn profile that listed me as a "Founder," I became more accepted and respected. The title made me feel like both more and less of an impostor.

But let's return to the parish hall at St. Luke's. We fielded so many questions including where we'd find children (partner agencies, shelters, and even public school referrals) and where we'd begin (the ground floor of St. Luke's) and how people could help.

"We believe it will cost us $200,000 to open the doors to the school next August. We've received," I announced, "a challenge from two individuals. These angel investors have agreed to donate two-thirds of that amount if we, as a community, can raise the other third."

"That's all?" shouted someone from the crowd. "We can do that easily."

And then the room filled with excited chatter and energy.

"I'll host a fundraiser," shouted someone in the back of the room.

"I'll take up a collection at my office," offered another attendee.

"I can take up a collection at my child's school," added another excited participant.

Everyone wanted to pitch in. The buy-in was immediate, but $67,000 was a lot of money to raise.

My husband jokes that during that time and over the next few years, we raised money by whatever idiomatic phrase is opposite of "death by a million cuts"—$67,0000 one penny at a time. Using St. Luke's as our fiscal agent, we began receiving donations of $10, $20, $100.

Throughout the next several months, people invited me into their homes and to their clubs and organizations to talk about our exciting project. I sent out email newsletters describing our progress. Our website alerted me each time we received a new donation. Each time an alert came through, I felt like a child at Christmas. I still remember the thrill I felt when I opened the message to see that someone who I didn't even know had donated $250 online. Apart from our angel investor, this was our largest single donation to date. The money just kept trickling in . . . small and steady.

Dollar by dollar, we inched toward our goal, but there were still people who doubted our ability to make this dream into a reality. There were still those who thought we were wasting time and money. There were even a few who began spreading the word that this project wasn't viable, and donors should beware. It was during these times that I was glad to have our original angel investor on my side. He knew everyone and was well respected in the community. He made several calls on behalf of the program to the naysayers in the community.

"You're welcome to your opinion," he told one philanthropist, "but there's no need to publicly derail this project."

We never received a dime from her foundation, but we also never heard another negative word. Thank goodness for the angels who were taking care of us. One step at a time, we were making the path together. It was hard work—the most difficult work I had ever done—yet every time we thought we had hit a dead end, a bend in the road would appear. We just kept taking the next step, one after another after another. Slowly things began to fall into place.

CHAPTER NINE
Change-Making

Only those who will risk going too far can possibly find out how far one can go.

–T. S. ELIOT

In the autumn of 2017, we formalized our board of directors and completed the paperwork for incorporation and nonprofit tax status. Our founding board consisted of six directors—the five women who began this fantastic journey and a recently retired attorney who had no idea what we had gotten him into until he was in too deep. Together, we strategized, submitted paperwork, developed budgets and organizational charts, built partnerships, raised money, and began the process of staffing. It was a whirlwind of activity.

The Boyce L. Ansley School would begin with a pre-kindergarten class of no more than fifteen scholars. We wanted to begin slowly. We believed this was our best path to success. Our plan was to hire one experienced social worker to support our families and two teachers to develop curriculum and lead the classroom. I had been clear from the beginning that I didn't want a full-time job that required me to be at the school every day. That sentiment had even been an entry on our initial strategic planning SWOT list. I needed to be in the community, so it was critical that we hire the right people to run the school's daily operations.

We posted our carefully written job descriptions on an online recruitment site, and within hours, we had hundreds of applicants. We were overwhelmed with both the number of applicants and the process of deciding who to bring in for an interview. Looking back, I'm proud of the work we did to identify staff for this groundbreaking project, but it was a difficult and sometimes comical process.

Our interviews took place in a conference room at St. Luke's just one floor above the future home of the school. One after another, candidates came and went. Some were inspiring and talented. Others were poorly prepared and disappointing. I was amazed at the number of applicants who came for interviews who didn't realize our school was just beginning. I was dumbstruck by the number of applicants who didn't know the school would serve children experiencing homelessness. There were applicants who just needed a job—any job—and applicants who longed to save the "poor children." We were committed to being a community that respected the dignity of every child and every family.

As one of my mentors said to me, "You're not starting a poverty petting zoo."

These were children and families who deserved to be seen as capable and special. The goal was not to be saviors. The goal was to enter into relationships and walk alongside families and children who were being left behind for no other reason than they were born into difficult circumstances.

Then we met Madeeha Rami.

"When I saw the job posting, I knew this was the place for me," said Madeeha in her interview.

Madeeha was a dark-skinned Muslim woman. She wore a hijab and carried herself with quiet dignity. Her résumé told the story of a well-educated and experienced teacher. Her interview introduced us to the rest of the package. As a Muslim who chose to cover her hair, Madeeha had lived discrimination and hate more times that she would like to count. She and her children had also lived through a period of insecure housing. She was strong and driven and yet had a tender understanding of the world. Her passion was teaching. Her goal was to discover the strengths and needs of each child and create individual learning plans.

She had taught a wide variety of children from a myriad of backgrounds. Early in our planning, we had created a list of core organizational values. At the top, we named that our staff be well-versed in teaching children with significant trauma and in modelling dignity and respect to both children and parents. Not only did Madeeha share our values, but she exhibited them in both her personal and professional life, as well. Our team loved her immediately. She understood what we were doing, and she was all in to make it a reality.

We rounded out our first staff with an assistant teacher and a social worker. The hiring and onboarding process were new to me, but my "get things done" personality served me well. I pulled in experts from our growing board and the community to assist with the process. St. Luke's agreed to employ our staff and contract them out to us. This allowed our small staff to opt in to a robust benefits package, and it allowed us to avoid the responsibility of payroll and all the accompanying paperwork. We simply paid the church each month.

In May of 2018, I convened our newly minted staff for our first meeting. We sat in tiny red plastic chairs at a tiny wooden table in what would become our first classroom. We introduced ourselves and discussed the philosophy of the program. We talked about expectations and ideas and of course, I created a to-do list with action steps and deadlines for each member of the team. I was excited and overwhelmed at the same time. There was still so much to do, and the countdown was on. We had a staff, but we didn't have students or curriculum or equipment. There was recruiting and training and shopping and fundraising and, and, and. We had a lot to do in a short amount of time.

We began reaching out to some of our partner agencies to initiate the recruiting process. In early June, we were invited to host a recruitment event at the Salvation Army housing facility. We had a banner, snack bags, and information about the new school. The plan was to staff a table in the lobby of the shelter from 5–7 p.m., as residents returned to the shelter for the evening. We were ready. We were excited. On the evening of the event, we arrived at the building in time to set up. There were four of us—three from the board and our newly hired social worker. We stood behind our table and waited.

What we didn't realize is that several other organizations would be in the lobby as well. The other tables offered housing assistance, job training, and various voucher programs. These were immediate needs. Parents rushed to these booths first. Their lines were long. The parents were desperate to secure services that could save their lives. School for the fall wasn't as much of a draw for parents of little ones. No one stopped at our table. We approached several families with children, but no one was interested. There were just too many other pressing needs. At 7 p.m., we took down our banner, gathered our snack bags and flyers and went home.

Panic consumed me as I exited the parking lot. I had failed. We had failed. How could we have been so wrong? We had raised over $300,000 that I would now need to return to the donors with gratitude and an apology for our failed project. My stomach turned, and my hands shook as I tried to navigate my way back home. The fear and shame that washed over me was heavy and deep. I thought I might actually drown. How would I return the money? What would I say? How would we figure it out? Tears ran down my face as I pulled up in front of my house.

My family's expectant faces fell when they saw me. I felt sick. I walked in the door and went straight up to my bedroom. My family gave me a moment of space and then quietly knocked on the bedroom door. They had been so excited for this step in the process. Their questions of "how many?" and "how cute?" were quickly changed to "what happened?" and "are you OK?"

"You're going to hit roadblocks," said my husband. "If this were easy, someone would have done it long ago."

"Don't give up yet," said my daughter.

"We're so proud of you, Mom," added my son.

I was touched by their support, but I went to bed stressed and confused. What if I had to return all the money? What about the staff I'd just hired? The scenarios played out repeatedly in my mind until I finally fell into a fitful sleep.

Surprisingly, I awoke the next morning feeling more hopeful. I knew in my heart that we were doing something big and necessary. I remembered a conversation I'd had with a friend at the start of this journey. She'd asked me if I knew the difference between "do-gooders" and "change-makers."

"A do-gooder," she explained, "is someone who does good until it gets complicated, but a change-maker stays with the task through the ups and downs because creating real change is never easy."

I wasn't in this to do a little good. I was in this to make a change in the world—to create a new path for an old problem. We could weather this storm and come out on the other side. We simply had to live through the hard days and tackle one problem at a time.

That morning, back in our tiny plastic chairs, we gave the teachers our disappointing update, and together, we brainstormed ways forward. Over the course of our research, we'd built relationships with many homeless-serving agencies. We simply needed to begin reaching out to more agencies for referrals.

I made several calls that morning and was able to set up several meetings and events. One after another, the outcome was the same. Some parents were interested, but no one was ready to commit. They had more immediate crises to face.

As I drove down to the smallest and most distant shelter on our list, I felt that sense of hopelessness beginning to build once again. My friend and fellow founding board member was with me. Both of us were feeling the pressure. It was hard to stay positive. This might be our last chance.

The case manager of the facility met us at the door and escorted us into a small office.

"Have a seat," she said. "I'll go call the women."

"Thanks," I said, already feeling a little unsure.

My friend and I sat in silence in the room. Beyond the closed door, we could hear children and women chatting and laughing. There were the sounds of dishes clanging and children playing. Dinner was ending and nightly chores beginning. After a few minutes, the case manager returned to the small office with five women—four were alone and one was accompanied by a young boy who sat on the floor and pulled out his toy cars.

"I hope it's OK I brought him," she said, gesturing to her son. "I didn't know I should find somebody to watch him."

"No problem," I said, smiling at the adorable child who was rolling a tiny car over my foot.

I asked his name and bent down to greet him on the floor. The moment I looked into his huge, innocent brown eyes, I remembered exactly why we had begun this journey. How could our community let this sweet child slip through the cracks? In his eyes and in his mother's face, I could see all the hopes and dreams for his future. They had lived in an apartment. He had been enrolled in pre-K at the neighborhood school, but the landlord failed to keep up with basic maintenance at their apartment. The building was finally condemned, and this precious child and his mother were left without a home. Here they were in a shelter far from their neighborhood—desperate and defeated.

I returned to my seat at the table, and my colleague and I introduced ourselves to the five mothers. We explained why we were there and described the program we were creating. We handed each mother the colorful informational flyer that we had prepared. It listed all the benefits of the school including uniforms, breakfast, lunch, school supplies, parent support, educational excellence, and before- and after-school care. The mothers turned over the flyers in their hands.

There was a moment of silence, and then one mother asked, "How much does it cost?"

"There's no cost to you," I explained. "It's fully funded by donors."

"Is there a test to get in?" asked another mother.

"No," I said. "We're accepting children who'll be four by September of this year. We're taking children on a first-come-first-served basis. There's a cap of fifteen students this year."

"Are you full? Is there room for my child?" one of the mothers asked.

The excitement and desperation in her voice took me by surprise.

"Of course," I said. "We have some forms right here, if you want to register."

"Do you have enough space for my child?" asked another mother.

I couldn't believe what I was hearing. I'm not sure who was more shocked and elated, the mothers who saw a new path for their children or my colleague and I who were beginning to think no one would want to come. One by one, each of the five mothers completed the registration form. There was an air of hope and excitement in the room coming from both sides of the table. We had just registered five students. I was at once overjoyed and completely humbled by the trust these women had in us. We were just two women who had shown up at their shelter with promises of a new path for their children. I was deeply honored that they trusted us to take care of their babies.

These women would become the backbone of our program. Their children would grow and blossom, and I would form bonds with them that would run the test of time. From that moment on, we were a team. We were in it together. It was truly a magical meeting.

In the days following our successful recruitment event, we registered six more students. One by one, agencies reached out to us with referrals. Our class was growing. We were on our way. On my desk sat the plaque that my daughter had given me only weeks earlier. "If your dreams don't scare you, they are not big enough."

CHAPTER TEN
Welcome to School

One child, one teacher, one book and one pen
can change the world.

–MALALA YOUSAFZAI

It was barely light when I arrived at St. Luke's on August 1, 2018. It was 6 a.m., and the sun was just peeking over the horizon. It was going to be a hot day—after all, it was August in Atlanta. The parking lot was empty and quiet. I parked in my regular spot and fished my new keys out of my bag while wrangling the helium balloons I had picked up to welcome our new scholars on their first day of school.

I unlocked the door to the church, turned off the alarm system (relief), and flipped on lights as I made way down to the ground floor. The classroom was so beautiful. Bright and airy and filled with colorful toys and blocks and crayons—everything a four-year-old could want or need in a new school. It even smelled like the first day of school—that familiar smell of pencil leads mixed with crayons and glue sticks. That smell always takes me back to all the first days of school in my own childhood when the possibilities were endless.

Just yesterday, most of the scholars and their families had come to meet their teachers, see their classroom, and pick up their uniforms, backpacks, and school supplies. There were eleven scholars registered for our inaugural pre-K class. Eight of them had come to the open house the day before and three of them we hadn't heard from since they registered. As I looked at the three backpacks hanging unclaimed on the hooks, I had a moment of sheer panic. What if no one showed up? Or what if they all showed up, and the teachers didn't come? Thankfully, the buzz of the door intercom interrupted my spiraling thoughts. All three members of our staff had arrived at the same time—excited and ready to conquer the day.

We scurried around reorganizing things that were already perfectly placed. We were all filled with nervous energy. We all had the same thought—"What if no one comes?"—and the same exhilaration—"This was really happening." Then, the sound of the intercom once again brought us back to reality.

It was 7:20 a.m. The doors would open at 7:40, and school would begin at 8. So why was the intercom buzzing at 7:20? The school staff were all here, and it was early for the church staff to arrive, plus they all had their own keys.

I walked to the front door, and there on the landing stood three young scholars in their new uniforms holding tightly to their parents' hands. I was supposed to set the precedent on this first day—the school opened at 7:40 a.m. This rule had come with much debate. Some parents requested drop-off as early as 6 a.m., and others had requested school not begin until later in the morning but stay open until 6 p.m. In the end, we agreed that the school day would run each day parallel to the public school hours—from 8 a.m. until 3 p.m. with early drop-off beginning no earlier than 7:40 a.m., and late pickup ending at 4 p.m. Oh—but their faces and their uniforms and their eagerness overwhelmed me. They were here. We had teachers and at least three young scholars. We were official.

I welcomed them into the building early and in my most official voice reminded them that going forward we would not open the doors before 7:40 a.m. We took family photos of the first day of school for each scholar and then said goodbye to the parents. Some parents were eager to move on and others were hesitant to leave. One father lingered in the classroom doorway. He was dropping off his twins. He looked sad and a little wild. He asked me if I would walk him back to the exit. Although we hadn't known each other long, I already felt a kinship with all the families. Our team was dedicated to honoring the dignity of each and every person who came through our doors. We were a team—the staff and the families. That was the backbone of the program. During the registration process, all the families had shared at least pieces of their stories and struggles. There was already a bond tying us all together.

"Ms. Kate," the father said. "I have to apologize. I've been drinking this morning. I woke up in a lot of pain today. I can't afford my medicine this month. And I'm so worked up about leaving my kids at school for the first time. I've never been away from them. I just needed a little drink to help, but then I thought you would smell it on me, and you might think I'm not a good dad, or you might call someone."

"Well," I said, "thanks for telling me. I can tell that you really love your twins. I remember when I left my kids at school for the first time. It was so hard. And I am sorry you can't afford to get your medicine right now. Maybe we can help you figure that out. Let's find time to talk. Please be careful and know that we'll always take good care of your babies. We're a team now—you, your wife, your twins, and the whole staff of the school. We're in this together."

"Thanks, Ms. Kate," he said, and we both had tears in our eyes. He hugged me then and walked away, pulling the rolling suitcase that held so many of his possessions. He and

I could not be more different, but over the course of the next several years—as his children grew and thrived—he and his wife became like family to me. I often imagine what they think when they see me. I hope they see a friend. I wonder what they think that I see when I look at them. I hope they know that I see a family who loves their kids fiercely and would do anything to see them succeed. I see heart and soul and courage. I see friends.

By the end of the first day, we had nine young scholars in our pre-K classroom: eight of the eleven who had preregistered and one who was referred by a social worker at a partner agency that very day. The whole day was a dream. There was singing and laughing and drawing. The entire classroom pulsed with an energy that can't even be described.

After time on the playground, the scholars returned to the room for lunch. The children stared at the feast with wide eyes. Some looked surprised, others confused, still others disgusted. The menu for the first day of school included crab cakes, whole peaches, salad, and multigrain rolls. This was definitely not your typical school lunch menu.

"What's this?" asked one scholar as he surveyed the plate.

As we were explaining the food set before them, a little girl picked up her peach and turned it slowly in her hand.

"This is a peach?" she asked. "I love peaches, but I've never seen this peach."

"Take a bite," I said.

She stared at the fruit a little longer and then looked at me like I was an alien.

"This isn't a peach," she said. "Peaches are in juice in a cup."

It was only then that we realized that whole fruit was a novelty. In the shelters and at the food banks, they receive canned fruit—diced peaches, fruit cocktail, applesauce. Whole fruit was not something the children encountered. We knew the crab cakes would be a new concept, but we didn't expect the fruit to be so unfamiliar.

They watched as we demonstrated how to bite into a peach. Before long, their beautiful faces were sticky and dripping with juice. They were giggling and chewing and experiencing the wonder of a new discovery. The crab cakes did not illicit the same overwhelming response, but all the scholars tried them, and some even declared the "fish thing" to be their new favorite food.

Figuring out food service had been a huge obstacle. Because we were so small, no one was interested in catering for us. We had committed to providing a balanced breakfast and lunch each day. It was important to the children's development. As the days wore on and the opening of the school neared, we still couldn't find a solution.

Then came Kenny.

We'd considered all options. A sorority at a nearby university had offered to share their midday meals with us if we picked it up. Several schools and catering services had offered to share both breakfast and lunch—if we picked it up. One organization was willing to drop off the meals, but we'd have to heat them and then clean and return all the dishes. With such a small staff, we knew that all of these options would be logistical nightmares.

Kenny was the part-time cook at St. Luke's. He worked only a few days each week preparing meals and hospitality for church events. One day in early July, our team had once more gathered to fret and brainstorm about our food-service roadblock. The start of school was rapidly approaching. We had to find a solution that would work. Someone suggested we ask Kenny. I was pretty confident that he wouldn't want to take on the daily responsibility or that we could afford to pay him enough to make it worth his time and effort. He'd have to commit to daily meal planning, shopping, and being at the church five days per week. It was a big ask, but we were running out of options and out of time.

I hadn't met Kenny, so the church staff connected us one day when he was in the church kitchen prepping for a reception. To my surprise, Kenny had been following the progress of the school and was quick to jump on board.

"I can't think of anything I'd like to do more than help with this program," he said through kind eyes and a broad smile.

Over the next weeks, we worked through logistics and meal planning. Kenny was determined to provide culinary opportunities (as he called them) that were above and beyond anything our scholars would receive at any other program. Breakfasts would consist of fruit and yogurt or oatmeal and cereal. Kenny would purchase the simple breakfast items and leave them in the refrigerator each evening for the teachers to set out in the morning. Lunch was where Kenny wanted to put his mark. He didn't want to make regular kid food—hot dogs, chicken nuggets, or fish sticks. Kenny wanted to create a menu that would expand their tastes and their nutrition. He wanted them to experience a truly different way of eating. Salad (which the scholars called "leaves") became a favorite side. Whole fruit was a part of each day's menu. Even when pineapple or watermelon was being served, Kenny would bring the whole fruit to the table and cut it right in front of the scholars. Surprisingly, crab cakes became a frequently requested meal along with hummus and carrots, chicken piccata, and vegetable soup. Not everyone liked every food, but they were always willing to try.

Kenny became a constant in their day—sitting and chatting with them for the entire lunch period. Kenny let the scholars help him measure out the portions for each plate, and he read books to them or just chatted with them while they ate. Mr. Kenny, as they called him, was their idol. His lunches were so legendary that church staff often appeared in the kitchen to see if there were leftovers. Kenny always made enough to pack and freeze leftovers to send home with the children and every now and then, a little extra for the staff. Lunch at The Ansley School was so much more than midday calories and nutrition. Lunch was another place to learn. Around the lunch table, the young scholars built social and academic skills. Their taste buds expanded, and their friendships grew.

Mealtime became so popular that church staff and community volunteers began asking to join us around the table. By the end of the first year, we had a robust volunteer program for both breakfast and lunch, giving the teachers a small break. Everyone loved the mealtime at The Ansley School—scholars and friends alike.

I look back now and can't imagine lunch without Kenny. Our meal program was just one more reason to believe that this school was divinely convened. Just when we thought a task was impossible, Kenny showed up and created something beyond our wildest expectations.

After lunch, the first day continued with much energy and fanfare. Every parent arrived pretty close to on time to pick up their young scholars. The children left with smiles and waves and lots of "see you tomorrows." We basked in the joy of an incredible first day, but in the back of my mind, I wondered if they would come back. This was our fear. This is what so many people cautioned us to expect. Transience would be the norm. Some would come for a week, we were warned, then be gone for a month, then come back for a month, then be gone for the year, but we could hope for the best. We had all the supports in place that we could provide. We just had to trust the process . . . and Kenny's lunch.

CHAPTER ELEVEN

Reality Hits

*The ultimate measure of a man is not where he stands
in moments of comfort and convenience, but where he
stands at times of challenge and controversy.*

—MARTIN LUTHER KING, JR.

Our fears were unfounded. The scholars did come back on day two and three and four. We enrolled a few more children, and by the end of the first month, we had eleven young scholars joining us every day for learning and lunching.

Near the end of the first month of school, our social worker organized a parent meeting to check in with our families. During the meeting, we asked them if there was anything that they thought wasn't working. At first no one spoke, but then one of the moms raised her hand.

"The white shirts are hard to keep clean," she said.

Our team had chosen the white shirts specifically because we thought they would be *easier* to keep clean with bleach. What we didn't consider is that laundry isn't as easy to do when you're without stable housing. Clothes are often worn multiple times between washings. Bleach and spot removers aren't easily available.

"What color do you think would be better?" our social worker asked.

"Something dark that doesn't show dirt. Navy-blue, maybe," responded a parent.

Our planning had been careful and thoughtful, but our team still had much to learn. We went to work to find new shirts.

When the monogrammed navy-blue uniform shirts arrived the following week, the parents were visibly stunned.

"No one ever cares what we think," said one mother.

What a realization. What a defining moment for our program. We were building a place where real community could grow. The parents were amazed that they had a voice and that their voices had been heard. Our team had a broader understanding of our families' struggles. From that day forward, we all worked hard to listen and learn and empathize with one another.

We continued to hold monthly parent meetings. We explained the curriculum and the expectations of each member of the scholar's team—parent, teacher, administration. We offered financial planning seminars, cooking classes, and even a "sips and strokes" day where the parents sipped on sparkling cider and painted their own masterpieces. Sometimes parents would offer to lead the meetings. One mother presented an entire session on "couponing." It was a huge hit. I think my favorite parent meeting, though, was the one where we created our own vision boards. "What's your dream for you and your children?" read the prompt on the wall. With scissors and glue sticks and stacks of magazines, parents created and presented their hopes for the future.

"This is the house that I want to buy for my family. See, there's a yard and a cute little dog," exclaimed one excited father, holding up his creation.

"This is a diploma because I want to go back to school and get a degree so I can be a good example to my children," shared a mother.

One by one, they each shared their hopes and dreams. The staff, too, created vision boards with similar aspirations. The universal goal in the room was that each of us, no matter where our journey had begun or led, wanted nothing more than a life filled with joy and family and friends.

Over the next months, the school continued to thrive, but my idea that I would have a flexible schedule and spend my time in the community raising funds was not what reality looked like. Our scholars and their families needed a lot of support. The parents had complicated lives with a lot of balls in the air all the time. They were always living on the edge of crisis. It's the nature of being without stable housing, and it's the reason we started the school in the first place. Our scholars, too, needed a lot of support. Most of them had never been in an organized social situation. They didn't know how to make friends, how to follow directions, how to sit "crisscross applesauce" on the rug, or line up and follow the leader. They all had significant trauma and needed support in figuring out how to express their emotions. Their language skills were low, and their emotional IQs were underdeveloped.

We thought we knew what to expect, but the reality of the situation was a surprise. In a mainstream school, a classroom teacher with eleven students and an assistant teacher could've managed to check the phone messages occasionally and to keep an eye on the day-to-day needs of the running a school. We did hire an intern to answer the phone and do some administrative tasks, but it was clear that someone with decision-making capabilities needed to be there to deal with the daily crises and turning points. We were a new program with high-need constituents. It required an all-hands-on-deck approach.

I don't remember ever making an intentional decision to be the one who would be present at the school every day.

It just happened. There was always something that needed to be handled. Someone had to be there to keep the ship afloat. So, between fundraising and running the daily operations and growing the program, I found myself at school all day long, every day. The founding board was supportive and present, but they all had lives and other jobs, and truthfully, I loved being at the school. I was passionate about what we were doing. I loved the scholars and their families with my whole heart. Most of all I was so proud of the work. I still felt like I was living in a dream.

I told myself (and my family who was used to having me at home) that I would put my all into the school until we had enough funding to hire an experienced head of school. I didn't take a salary because it would just be more money I would need to raise. It was a huge job. Not only was I serving as president and head of school, I was also the chair of the board of directors, but, again, I was in love with everything about this program. It had become as much a part of me as my own family. I couldn't imagine *not* being in the center of the growth. So, day after day, I worked. The scholars thrived, and the school grew more and more stable. The community we were creating was beautiful. It wasn't without bumps and complications, but we were moving forward.

I wish I could say that the community we built inside the school immediately spread outside our walls, but the reality proved to be a little more complicated than that.

St. Luke's is an outreach-oriented, socially progressive church. Outside the walls of the church building, poverty and food and housing insecurity are realities. The church spends a great deal of time and energy out in the neighborhood trying to give voice to the voiceless and support to the underserved. Occasionally, someone from the streets would wander into the building, but mostly, the building was insulated from the neighborhood, that is, until the school opened. Suddenly, the building was filled with strangers—at least that is how it felt to the church staff. Mothers and fathers would bring their children to school and then use the bathroom to change and wash up for the day. Parents with nowhere to go would make themselves comfortable for the day in church sitting areas. Some parents would nap on the sofas in the reception area. We tried to strike a balance between being hospitable and creating boundaries, but it was difficult— especially on rainy days when our parents had nowhere else to seek shelter.

The church staff was uncomfortable. They felt unsafe having strangers in and out of the building. Violence was a reality in the neighborhood, and the church staff felt at risk with people who they didn't know wandering in and out all day. We created a check-in system for parents to use when entering the building, but it wasn't easy. There were so many people coming and going and with them came the drama of the life of someone struggling to survive day-to-day.

Our pre-K room was a large and bright space on the ground floor of the church building. The floor-to-ceiling windows provided all the light but also provide an unobstructed view of gang activity and violence taking place on the Courtland Street corridor. One day, late in the year, the scholars were just settling in for their afternoon rest time. The mats were laid out on the floor and each child had picked one book or toy to keep with them while they rested. Their shoes were placed neatly at the end of their mats. The lights were dim, and we were entering that lovely but short period of quiet and calm. The staff needed the break as much as the scholars.

Suddenly, two uniformed police officers entered the classroom and rushed to the windows. The children immediately began crying and screaming. Chaos broke out. Some scholars were cowering in the corner. Some were frozen in place, and others took off down the hall. The officers, unaware of the activity in the room, were on their radios communicating with a team of officers outside. The staff was trying to gather and comfort the children, and I was trying to figure out what was happening. Within a minute, the officers put away their radios and began to head back to the exit.

"Excuse me," I said. "What's happening here?"

"Oh, sorry ma'am," one of the officers responded. "We had a report of a drug deal going down on the street, and we were trying to get the best vantage point."

"Do you know this is a school?" I asked. "Who let you in here?"

"We cleared it with the main office upstairs," responded the officer as he took the stairs toward the exit. "Sorry for the inconvenience."

What was happening? My first priority was calming our traumatized young scholars and our staff. Their panic was real and deep. They were crying and shaking. Then one young boy spoke through his sobs.

"The police came to my place and took my daddy away. I haven't seen him. My mommy says he'll come home soon, but I don't know where he is."

One by one, the children began sharing their experiences with the police.

"The police came to my street last night, and there was lots of gun shots."

"My mommy told me to put my hands up when I see the police."

"The police took my sister away."

These young children who lived on the streets had experienced a world—in their four short years of life—that I knew nothing about. I only knew what I saw on the news from the comfort of my own home. To me, the police were our protectors. To these young children, the police were the ones who came and ripped their families apart.

"The boy who stays next to me was laying on the ground in his blood with his hands tied behind his back. The ambulance took him away, and he never came back," said one frightened girl.

We spent the rest of the afternoon comforting and talking to the children. Therapists from one of our community partners specializing in trauma and mental health care came to support us as we calmed the children and spoke with their parents. Once the situation with our families was under control, I went to the church office.

"Did you know that the police just came down to the school and barged into a classroom?" I asked the first person I saw in the office.

"No," she responded. "What are you talking about?"

I explained what happened and together we determined that the officers had entered the building and alerted the substitute receptionist that they needed access to the downstairs window. She figured since they were uniformed officers, that it would be OK, and she allowed them entrance. Apparently, this wasn't the first time that officers had entered the building to gain a vantage point on crime in the area. Typically, this wouldn't be a problem, but now that the lower floor was filled with young children, we needed some new protocol.

That afternoon, I reached out to the commander of the area police zone. He couldn't have been more apologetic and responsive. I explained to him my concern over the reaction and the trauma of our scholars and families. Together, we made a plan to build a better community between police officers and our Ansley families. For the remainder of the year, the zone-five officers came each week to be with our scholars. They read stories, played games, and answered questions. I stood back in wonder as we forged new ways of being together. There is still much work to be done, but the friction created with and through our little school created a spark for change and growth in so many places and so many ways.

CHAPTER TWELVE
Unexpected Loss

Her absence is like the sky,
spread over everything.

–C. S. LEWIS

In April of 2019, the axis upon which my life rotated shifted forever. My husband and I and two of our children were on a much-needed beach vacation. It was spring break, and school was closed for the week. The morning was clear and bright. My husband and I rose with the sun and hiked down the beautiful white sand beach to where a coral reef anchored just offshore. The area was usually crowded and chaotic, but at this early hour, we were the only visitors. With snorkel gear in place, we explored the outer edges of the reef. The sun reflected off the blue water and a world of color and life opened before us. I love to snorkel. The quiet and peace of the underwater world refreshes my body, my mind, and my soul.

An hour later, we emerged from the water just in time to see our children sauntering down the beach in our direction to join us for breakfast. With snorkel gear, towels, and sandy damp clothes covering our very wet swimsuits, we went to the nearby beach café—famous for fluffy coconut-banana pancakes. Everything about the morning was perfect, and I bathed in the joy of the day.

When we returned to the condo, full and happy, I noticed a couple of missed calls from my sister. I sat on the edge of my bed and called her back. She answered on the first ring.

"Sister," she said immediately in the familiar way we referred to each other, "are you by yourself?"

"Well, sort of—the family is here with me," I said.

"Mom died."

The words hit me like a dagger. My head was reeling. I must have heard her wrong. My dad was the sick one. My mom was the caretaker. My dad had severe dementia and mobility issues. My dad was the one recovering from the "widow-maker" heart attack that he had suffered just a few weeks earlier.

"She must mean Dad," I thought.

"Sister," she said interrupting my haze. "Say something."

"Wait, what?" I said, trying to make sense of the conversation.

"Mom died in her sleep. I'm here with Dad."

My dad, who couldn't get out of bed without assistance, had awoken to find Mom unresponsive. Before his series of strokes and subsequent dementia, my dad had been a brilliant doctor. He said he knew when he awoke and saw her that she was dead. He somehow managed to dial 911, get out of bed, dress himself and navigate the stairs to his favorite chair in the den before the ambulance arrived. Our mom, the healthy one—the lively one—the caretaker of us all—had somehow died in her sleep.

I felt sick. I couldn't breathe.

"Can I talk to Dad?" My voice sounded much sturdier than I felt.

There was a quiet commotion as she handed the phone to our dad.

"Dad," I said, trying not to cry. "Are you OK?"

"Yes, I'm OK," he said in his matter-of-fact voice. "There are a lot of people here with me. Someone has made me some toast. I'm going to eat it now."

"OK Dad. I'm on my way. I love you," I said.

My husband was already busy on his phone booking me a plane ticket home.

"I'm coming home," I told my sister. "I'll be at the house tonight. Are you OK? What's happening?"

"We are just sitting here waiting for you to come home and make a plan," responded my sister.

In their everyday lives, both my sisters are smart, strong, and successful, but when we're together, the birth order trumps it all. I'm the oldest. I'm the one who should have all the answers. Only this time, I had no ideas. I showered quickly and caught the shuttle from our hotel to the airport. It was a hot day, and the shuttle was full. I sat next to the window, watching the passing scenery through my tears—beach, sand, sky, palm trees. I was lost in a flood of grief, confusion, and fear. What were we going to do? How was this happening?

The airport was small, hot, and crowded. There was no room inside, so I stood crying and sweating in the open-air reception area. I wanted to call someone, but I didn't know who. I wanted to talk to someone, but I didn't know what I wanted to say. My sisters were waiting at home for me to come and make a plan. What was I going to say? I had absolutely no idea. I wasn't even sure I could do this.

I guess at some point, the announcements called me to board my flight. I remember very little about the journey to Atlanta. I was frozen—in shock. I just sat still, upright, staring straight ahead for the three-hour trip back to Atlanta where I was greeted by an extra-long, extra-crowded customs entry line. Only then did I begin reaching out. I texted one of my priests:

"My mom died last night. I'm at the airport. She was my father's sole caregiver. I don't know what we're going to do."

Even though it was Saturday evening, her reply came back quickly and washed over me like balm.

"I'm here for you. Take a deep breath. You're not alone."

We exchanged a few messages about my next steps and ended our conversation with the promise that I would reach out when I arrived in my hometown of Birmingham. Feeling a little more grounded, I texted two friends as I inched along in the slow-moving queue. Both responded almost immediately and with great comfort and love. My neighbor balked at my comment that I was going to call a ride service to bring me home. She jumped in her car and drove the thirty minutes from our neighborhood to the airport to shuttle me home. Friendship and love were my saving graces that horrible day.

The plan was for me to land in Atlanta, go home, repack, and make the two-and-a-half-hour drive to Birmingham that night, but when I got home, I was awash in sadness and fatigue. My sisters, who were already at our childhood home with our dad, encouraged me to spend the night at home and make the drive the following morning. More grace and love in our communal distress.

I tossed and turned all night, and then I rose with the sun to make the last leg of the long journey. The drive was uneventful, and I arrived in Birmingham just before 8 a.m.

Surprisingly, though not so surprisingly, our father insisted we go to church. Liturgy and theology, practice and faith, those were the foundations of our dad's life, and through him, the foundations for mine. I couldn't imagine how we would navigate so many well-wishers through our raw edges. I couldn't imagine how we would navigate the wheelchair and the transfers and the suit and tie, but I also couldn't imagine *not* going to be with those who loved us most as we practiced our faith during this tremendously dark time. And so, we helped Dad dress, navigated the transfers and the wheelchair and the confusion, and found solace in the liturgy of the Word and the people who were like family to my parents.

During the week that followed, our dad was uncharacteristically alert and self-sufficient. He was able to engage in some conversations. He greeted those who stopped by with hospitality and warmth. It was as if he knew we needed him. When he was napping or with his caregiver, my sisters and I spent hours talking through details and trying to make a plan. We listed all the possibilities for next steps with Dad and began to fill in pros and cons for each. Our one rule was that "guilt" could not be on the list because no matter what we decided, we were going to feel guilty. If we made him move home with one of us, if we left him here alone with hired caregivers, if we found him an assisted-living facility, all of those choices would come with feelings of guilt . . . so that was a given and off the table.

No one prepares you to care for an aging parent. The role reversal is heartbreaking. My parents made me who I was. We didn't always agree, but through their presence and their love, I grew to be the woman I had become. Our mom was still making decisions for herself. She was taking care of Dad. It felt right for her to make those hard decisions for herself and her spouse, but now our dad needed his girls to provide care, and we weren't sure we were ready for the assignment.

We powered through the best we could, and by the end of the week, with the funeral service quickly approaching, we had settled on a plan that we felt was the best we could offer. Dad was doing so well. He seemed to understand all that was happening and all that needed to happen. He had opinions (which was not uncommon) on the final arrangements, and he balked at the idea that we go to the bank and put our names on his checking accounts. It was nice to have our dad back in a tiny way in the midst of our loss.

The day of the funeral, Dad woke and dressed himself with little assistance. We stood with him and greeted well-wishers and friends for ninety minutes before heading into the sanctuary. My sisters and I stood on either side of Dad during the service as we noticed his balance and strength weakening. It had been a long day. By the time the service was over, Dad was shaking. The grief had finally overcome him, but as we were guiding him back into his wheelchair and beginning the journey to the car, one of my sisters looked at him and said,

"Look at his face. I think he may be having a stroke."

This could not be happening, but while I was trying to convince myself and my sisters that he was simply grieving—finally—they were already calling 911.

A "catastrophic" stroke was how the doctors in the ER described it. He shouldn't be alive. He wanted to die when Mom died. It would have been a blessing in so many ways. Theirs was a love story for the ages. "Bette and Crawford"—"Crawford and Bette"—no one ever said their names separately. They were perfectly knit together, yet Dad was stubborn, and he was worried about his girls. He loved us voraciously. He refused to die.

We spent the next ten days with him in ICU. I was a mess. I was stressed about my dad. I was stressed about my family in Atlanta. I was stressed about my parents' house and finances. I was stressed about the school. And I missed my mom so, so deeply.

Taking a week away from the school for spring break had been hard for me. There was money to raise and partnerships to build and staff to support. So, the fact that I was now heading into my fourth week away from the school was only adding to my load. I had taken the first week after spring break completely disconnected. I put a message on my email that I had a family emergency, and the board of directors would handle all needs. I decided that if the program couldn't stay afloat if I took a couple of weeks off then so be it.

During the third week of my absence, when my dad was resting in ICU, I began communicating with staff and answering emails. I was doing all that I could to keep things moving forward, but I wasn't there, and things were falling through the cracks. I felt pulled in so many directions. Some members of the board had reached out to me to let me know that the board thought that I should step down. There was another board member who would take my role. I had too much on my plate, they explained, so it might be time for me to back down and give someone else the day-to-day leadership.

I had given my heart and soul to this project. It had become part of me. Maybe I was being too possessive. Maybe I was holding on too tightly. Looking back now, I can see my tightening grip on the program, but no one had given it as much time and effort and dedication as I had. I had sacrificed my whole life for this program, and so that call caught me completely off guard and brought me only anger and deeper despair. The offer wasn't for someone to step in and help me. The offer was to replace me, I dug in and stood firm and stubborn.

I have reflected on this moment a lot. For a while, I was angry and scared. Then I was mad and indignant. Then I was guilt-ridden and ashamed, but now, with some distance and perspective, I understand this moment as the beginning of the end. I claim my role in holding on too tightly, but I refuse to accept that it was all my fault. I understand now that whatever miscommunications or mistranslations led to my exit from the program began on this day.

CHAPTER THIRTEEN

A Beloved Community

*Your great mistake is to act the drama
as if you were alone.*

–DAVID WHYTE

"Take a look around you," I said to a room full of young scholars. "Look beside you. Look behind you. Look in front of you."

We were in the parish hall at St. Luke's. It was the last day of our first year of school. Our eleven scholars sat in grown-up-sized folding chairs on the front row. At my direction, they began to twist and turn in their chairs, looking all around the room. All around them, the room was filled with parents, siblings, aunts, uncles, donors, friends, church staff, community partners, and the staff and teachers who had become their everyday constants.

"No matter where you go in your life," I continued, "these people will always have your back. Never forget that you are part of a community that loves and supports you today and always. You'll never have to be alone."

The ceremony was more than I could have ever dreamed. After I spoke, the scholars performed a scene from Shakespeare's *A Midsummer Night's Dream* that they had prepared through our ongoing partnership with a Shakespeare company up the street. After the bows and applause, the scholars treated the room to a song and dance they had choreographed themselves. The audience went wild. I stood back in sheer wonder, struck by the magnitude of the year. We had all come so far and learned so much. All of our lives had been forever changed.

After the performances, the room settled. One by one, each of the young scholars marched over a small wooden bridge set up on our makeshift stage. On the other side of the bridge, they received a certificate of completion and a big hug from their teachers and parents. At the reception and picnic that followed, we took photos with parents and scholars while we feasted on hot dogs, hamburgers, and popsicles. It was a glorious day. We had made it through one year of this wild journey. It was a wonderful celebration for all.

As the room was clearing and it was time for the staff to begin their much-needed summer break, one of our teachers pulled me aside and presented me with a small gift bag. Inside the bag was a tiny metallic globe with the note that read: "I believe you will start schools like this all over the world, and I will help you."

Never more deeply had I ever felt such a stark mix of emotions. This school was one of the greatest joys and journeys of my life. I was constantly in awe of our families and the obstacles they had to overcome each day just to keep going. We had created a beloved community. I was overwhelmed with gratitude and wonder every day. But I was drowning. I was drowning in grief over the loss of my mom and the absence of my dad. The sadness had settled on my shoulders like a giant boulder that felt like it might crush me at any moment. I was overwhelmed with exhaustion. I couldn't sleep. My blood pressure was high, and I had lost more than ten pounds off my already small frame. I was trying to be everything to everyone—my family, the scholars, the funders, the board. I was killing myself, and yet here we were. The only thing I knew to do was to keep moving. Looking back, I wish I had known how to ask for help.

The Enneagram is an ancient form of personality typology. What I like most about the system is that it recognizes how the unique threads of our personalities can be both our greatest gifts and our deepest struggles. On the Enneagram, I am absolutely a textbook "three"—also known as "the achiever." According to the Enneagram Institute, "threes are self-assured, attractive, and charming. Ambitious, competent, and energetic, they can also be status-conscious and highly driven for advancement. They are diplomatic and poised but can also be overly concerned with their image and what others think of them. They typically have problems with workaholism and competitiveness." A three at her best is a role model. A three at her worst fears being seen as worthless.[7]

This description could not fit me more perfectly. During those frantic and overwhelming days in the spring of 2019, I was at once the best kind of "three"—successful, getting it all done, making real change—and the worst kind of "three"—crushed and overwhelmed without the ability to truly find support. The conversation with board members during my time away after the death of my mom kept replaying in my head. It had ignited my deepest fear that I wasn't adding value, that I wasn't useful.

For the last few months, I had been holding on to the idea that a summer break was all I needed to get myself together. We had partnered with the YMCA to provide summer care for our scholars. The program would allow parents continuous childcare. The scholars would continue their journey of academic and social development, and the school staff and I would get our much-needed break.

Summer flew by, and we all returned feeling refreshed and reenergized. The church staff had cleaned the space and waxed the floors. We had gained access to a couple more rooms on the ground floor so we could accommodate our growing staff and our new class of scholars. As planned, our original pre-K scholars moved up to our new kindergarten class, and we welcomed a new class of pre-K children into the program. We began year two with every one of our original scholars plus new friends in both our kindergarten and pre-kindergarten classes. Our roster more than doubled as we counted twenty-five young and eager scholars on our rolls.

Unlike the first year, we didn't have to go out searching for students. All our new families were referred by our current families and our community partners including the public school system. Our reputation in the community was growing. During our first year, we had proven our program to be solid and impactful. The referrals, though, exposed a sobering reflection of our community. One referral, in particular, caught our attention.

Ann had spent her five years of life bouncing between shelters. In Georgia, we have a state funded pre-kindergarten program. Each year, children are admitted or denied access through a lottery system. Children whose parents can afford to pay tuition for a private pre-K option can choose that route if they are denied through the lottery or just prefer a private program. Children without resources are out of luck when they don't "win the pre-K lottery."

Ann's mother had applied for Ann's entrance into a state pre-K program, and Ann had won a spot. Her mom was thrilled that her daughter would be able to begin her academic journey so early. She dreamed of her daughter excelling in school and maybe, one day, having a chance to be the first person in their family to go to college. The reality was that Ann, like so many children without stable housing, entered the program without age-appropriate academic or social development. As we had seen with our first class of pre-K scholars at The Ansley School, Ann needed extra support in school. Ann's teachers did what they could to support her, but with so many other students learning at so many different levels the process was difficult. End-of-the-year testing showed that Ann wasn't prepared for kindergarten. This was a common occurrence with no real solution. Since the program was a lottery system, children couldn't simply repeat the grade. Most of the time, the children were promoted to kindergarten with the hope that they would soon catch up with their peers. Most of these children never catch up. It's a well-reported fact that until the third grade, teachers teach children to read. Beyond the third grade, teachers teach children *through* reading. If a child isn't reading at grade level by the end of third grade, their chances of success are slim. Without special attention and extra support, many children find themselves in this exact situation.[8]

It was the homeless liaison at the public school system who reached out to me one day just days before school began.

"I want to discuss a referral with you," she said.

It's common in a public school system for the homeless liaison to have up to a thousand students on their case load. When parents enroll their children in school, there is a box to check if unstable housing is an issue. The homeless liaison's job is to support these families as they navigate their way through the system. It's a tough situation for both the families and the liaison. The needs of these families are so great. The paperwork is all-consuming, and the crises are never-ending. With such a large case load, it's impossible to keep every child from falling through the cracks.

On this hot summer morning, the homeless liaison at the school system decided to try something new.

"We have a student without housing who didn't perform well in our pre-K program this year. She's bright, but she needs more specialized attention. Would it be possible for her to transfer to your program to repeat pre-K?"

"Absolutely," I said.

This is exactly why we started this program and why we kept it privately funded. We weren't competing with the public school; we were partnering to find the best solutions for the children in our community.

Ann enrolled, and she thrived. She was a leader in the pre-K class. Her skills, though not ready for kindergarten, were more advanced than our other entering scholars. She gained confidence and the extra attention she needed to strengthen her development. By the middle of her first year at our school, Ann was splitting her day between our pre-K and kindergarten classes. She could have transferred back to the public school at the end of the year, but her family was sold on our small, specialized school, and they stayed. Over the years, we continued to refer children back and forth between the public school system and our private program. The public school system was even able to share some federal funding they received for students who transferred to our program. It was the beginning of a beautiful partnership built to fill a gaping need.

The families who referred new students to us revealed a different problem growing in our community. Many of the referrals were cousins of our students—that means that sisters or brothers who grew up struggling continued to struggle in the next generation. While it was fun for our scholars to go to school with their cousins, the prevalence of generational poverty in our community could not be ignored.

In the 1970s and 1980s, St. Luke's had housed a street academy to serve students from Atlanta Public Schools who were struggling in the traditional school setting. The program later became Communities in Schools—the nation's leading dropout prevention organization. In its days as an alternative school on the campus of St. Luke's, two of our current school parents had attended. They hadn't kept in touch but were reunited when both of their children enrolled in The Ansley School. Both had come from difficult situations and were now doing all that they could to find a way for their children to experience a different outcome.

Both parents who had attended the street academy shared their academic journey and their hopes for their children.

Brianna, one of those parents, was a particularly vocal and enthusiastic advocate for The Ansley School. She loved the community we had built and the fact that we loved her children so much. One day her son got into a fight with another student. When Brianna came to pick him up, she had tears in her eyes. It wasn't the first time that her son had had a violent outburst at school, and she assumed she would need to find him a new school. She was angry and frustrated. She entered the building yelling down the hall at her son.

"What were you thinking?" she yelled before she had even entered the office. "This is such a good opportunity for you, and you're throwing it away."

When she rounded the corner to enter the office, she stopped short. Her son was sitting calmly with several staff members, and they were all talking.

"Hey—it's OK. It wasn't nice for you to hit your friend. It hurt him," said a teacher.

"But I was mad," said the young boy.

"Will you let us help you find other ways to show when you're mad?" asked another teacher. "We have lots of cool ways to get out your mads."

Together the teachers and the boy walked down the hall and back into a classroom.

"Are you kicking us out?" asked Brianna.

"No," I said. "We'll just need to work together to find ways to help your son release his anger in a better way. We love your son, and we want him to stay right here with us in this school. He is doing so well."

"I used to fight a lot, and I got kicked out of a lot of schools. That's how I ended up at the street academy, but I never even graduated," she said.

"We're a team here with you and your son. We won't leave you stranded," I said.

Her relief was immediate, and tears filled her eyes.

"No one has ever had our backs before," she said. "Thank you."

Months later at a parent meeting, Brianna related a story to the other parents.

"My friend asked me why I work so hard to get my kids all the way to The Ansley School when I could just put them on the bus near the shelter," she announced. "I tell them,

'The Ansley School is our family. Rain, snow, sleet, or hail, I'm taking my kids to that school until they kick them out for college.'"

These families were truly stuck with little support in getting up and out of their situation. Generations of their families had struggled in the abyss of generational poverty, but they were fighting for something different for their children. I hoped that just maybe our program could offer a new way out.

CHAPTER FOURTEEN

New Ways of Being

May your choices reflect your hopes,
not your fears.

–NELSON MANDELA

"I know they say we shouldn't hug, but I'm so glad to see you. Do you mind?" said my colleague as I entered her new office.

Her organization had been such a help to us as we navigated creating our new school. It was February of 2020, and we were meeting to catch up on how things were going. COVID was just beginning to bear its ugly teeth. Although we had no idea what lay ahead, the culture was already shifting. Hand sanitizer was showing up everywhere, and the idea of "social distancing" was just emerging in the media.

"It's fine," I said. "It's been a long time."

Then, as was typical in these days, our conversation quickly turned to COVID.

"I hear the public schools may close before the end of the year," shared my colleague.

"I heard that, too," I said. "That's the advantage of being a small, private school. We can stay open even if they need to close. They're so big, and I'm sure it gets complicated. I can't imagine a scenario where we'd need to close our doors."

Our conversation turned to the progress we were making and the funding we were securing. It was constant work, but so far, everything was going well. The scholars were thriving. Testing showed that their academic and social development was improving. The board had approved hiring an experienced principal to co-lead the school with me. I would still be in charge of strategy, vision, and fundraising, but the principal would handle all day-to-day operations and manage the staff. I was nervous but excited.

We had also just signed a lease on a new space. We'd be adding a first grade in the next year with new scholars and new staff. We just didn't have enough room to grow in the church. In the familiar way that I'd always felt the school to be divinely convened, we stumbled upon a building just across the street from the church. It was an office building that had been converted into a church. Recently the church had relocated to a larger building. The new owner of the building had leased the upstairs office space but was having difficulty finding a tenant for the lower level. A friend in the real estate business had shared the listing link with me.

The email read:

Look at this. It must be divine intervention.

I immediately clicked on the link and was floored by what I found.

The space had been the children's area of the church. It was brightly painted and included large classrooms, a small auditorium, bathrooms with children-sized toilets, and its own exterior entrance. There was a bus stop right at the building entrance. There could not be a better scenario. The move would be easy for our families and, wow—to be in our own space with room to grow and create was a dream. I was instantly sold.

It was perfect, but with rent (something we didn't currently have), a principal's salary (another new and large expense), and a new class of scholars, our budget would almost double. That was a lot of money to raise, but, in that moment, I felt exhilarated by the challenge and the future.

Change-making is never easy. I was now fully aware of this, but these bold steps were the path to a sustainable program with true staying power.

"This is truly inspiring," said my colleague as we wrapped up our conversation. "I know it won't be easy."

"But do you think it's possible?" I asked. "We're taking a big step."

"This whole project has been one big step after another," she said, "but look where you are. I've been in this industry a long time, and what you're doing is groundbreaking."

We had assembled the best team of community partners. I felt confident that the future was bright for the school and for the scholars. I left the meeting feeling a sense of peace and joy. This was really working. The reality was still a surprise to me every day.

Back at the school, all was calm. I checked in with the staff and then settled in at the folding card table set up in the corner of the room designated as the school office. The social worker and intern had small workspaces in the room. They were both engrossed in projects, which was good because I had a lot to tackle. I needed to finalize several reports before our upcoming board meeting.

The decision to hire a principal had not been easily discerned. I'd been working with the board to develop a new organizational chart. We strategized and consulted with experts to create a structure that made sense. We also refined our five-year budget projections to include our new expenses and growth estimates.

"You need to decide if you want to stay on as staff or board chair," one of our directors had said at our last meeting.

The comment had given me pause. I was tired, and I knew I couldn't do this forever, but I also didn't know how to not do it. Proper governance had been a priority of ours since the beginning. That is one reason I believe we were able to get some of our earliest funding. We were dotting all our i's and crossing all our t's. It gave funders confidence in our organization. A director on the board could serve three three-year terms. I was about to complete my first term. If I gave up my staff position, I would have to leave the school in only six short years. That scared me. If I stayed on as staff, I was agreeing to remain the person at the end of the line whose responsibility was to handle everything when others weren't available. Technically, we were all volunteers, but I was the one who was always accountable. From reconciling the petty cash to substituting for a sick teacher, I was the one who got the job done. Others came in to volunteer when they were able. For me, that wasn't an option. It was the nature of the position that I had assumed. I loved it, and I hated it at the same time.

I had asked the board if I could take some time to think about my answer. I spent the next week writing down everything that I did and trying to create a job description for my role. My duties were far and wide. This was not yet a job designed for an official hire. Then I created a pros and cons list for my staff role and my board role. It's hard to admit, but the word "ego" showed up on the list a lot.

"I just don't know what to do," I said to the executive committee.

"Well, it's your call," one responded.

"I've written down all the things I do to keep the school running and growing. I don't see how we can find one person passionate enough to take all of this on with what we can afford to pay," I said.

I had shared my list with the group. It included everything from raising our million-dollar budget each year to managing the staff and keeping our building up and running. Then there were the "soft duties" that included supporting families who were living from crisis to crisis each and every day.

"What if we hired someone to take some of the day-to-day management off of your plate?" asked one of the small group.

And just like during our earliest days of collaborating and dreaming about the school, a plan began to emerge. The room filled with a familiar energy of collaboration. After some discussion and visioning, we decided that we would hire a principal to handle the day-to-day operations and educational philosophy of the school. They were unsure, but I still felt that we would need a staff person to drive fundraising and strategy. In the end, it was decided that the best course of action was for me to roll off the board of directors and function as staff until we were settled enough to know what we needed.

"I want the new principal to report to the board," I said. "I'm not an educator. I would have no idea how to manage a principal."

We had several experienced educators on our board, and so it was agreed. Both the principal and I—as president and founder—would report to the board. I was energized by our plan. I was hopeful that the new structure would allow me to have more flexibility and focus on the parts of the job that suited me. I was still a little unsure about giving up my role as a board member. But, from the beginning, we had worked to create sound governance, and this move was by the books.

The day of our interviews, I was filled with a mix of thrill and anxiety. The right principal would be a game changer. We hired a firm to assist with the hiring process and put together an outstanding search committee. It was important that our academic program was stellar. That is what we promised our funders and our families. I could only take it so far, but an experienced educator could take us to the next level. That was my ultimate dream, but deep down inside, I was afraid. This school meant more to me than anything I had ever done. What if the new hire didn't really understand our vision? What if we couldn't find the right person for the job?

I knew I needed to let go a little, but I had sacrificed so much for this project. I wanted someone to take some of the load, but deep down, I wasn't really sure I knew how to give it away. I thought I was keeping my anxiety buried, but as we sat in the conference room waiting for our first applicant to arrive, one of the board members who was a prominent educator and a dear friend leaned over to me and whispered, "Breathe." I didn't even realize I was holding my breath.

"You're doing a great job, and we're going to find someone who's perfect for this position," she whispered. "Now—please relax and breathe. We've got your back."

It's a trite phrase, but in that moment I felt seen, and a little calmer—until the first candidate walked into the room.

"Welcome," I said as we all took turns shaking hands. "We're so glad you're taking time to talk with us."

"Thank you," she said. "I'm so excited about the opportunity."

"Can you describe your educational philosophy?" asked one of our committee members.

"Well," she began, "I think that it's always best to establish who is in charge in the classrooms."

She went on to explain how rigid discipline and structure were the best ways to keep children focused and learning.

"If you allow children too many choices, the classroom turns into a playground rather than a place for learning," our candidate continued.

The committee members and I exchanged glances. This was not our educational philosophy. Our website was very clear about our focus. We met our scholars where they were. Our teachers were trained in a multitude of learning styles to take into account trauma and cultural differences. She wasn't the right person for the job, but it was our first interview, and we were unsure how to end it so quickly. So, for the next twenty minutes, we sat and listened to exactly what we did not want. Unfortunately, as the day proceeded, we had several opportunities to hone our skills at cutting interviews that were dead end.

"I've never worked with inner-city children, but my daughter has a black friend," shared our next candidate.

I had to stare down my colleague across the table and silently will her not to explode.

The morning continued to be disappointing, and our break for lunch could not have come early enough. We ate mostly in silence. I think we were all a little frustrated and tired, but we were determined. We wouldn't hire anyone who wasn't the right person for the job even if we had to start the search again.

After lunch we had several other mediocre candidates. When our 3 p.m. appointment came in, we were prepared for another round of frustration. Little did we know that our luck was about to change.

"I just repatriated from seven years abroad," our next candidate explained. "I built an international school for young boys. Before that I built a Montessori school in the States. Our time overseas was up, and we have family in Atlanta, so we moved here."

Kimberly Andrews's educational philosophy was a perfect match for our goals, and she had history to back up her beliefs. Her energy was incredible. I could tell from the mood in the room that we had found not just a quality candidate but possibly the perfect candidate. As I drove home from the long and stressful day, I felt a sense of peace wash over me. I had a good feeling. I really liked her. This was going to work.

The next week Kimberly came to the school to meet the staff and complete her paperwork. She and I sat in a large church conference room just one floor above the classrooms. As she signed the documents, we talked about plans and goals. We just clicked. We were going to make a great team. In our excitement, neither of us could possibly anticipate the enormity of the threat that was looming.

On Thursday, March 12, 2020, as I sat in that conference room with Kimberly, Atlanta Public Schools announced that due to the growing COVID crisis, beginning Monday, March 16, all system schools would close for at least two weeks.

"Sorry to interrupt, but have you heard?" Our school social worker poked her head into the conference room. "Atlanta Public Schools have decided to suspend school."

The news was shocking, but I remained adamant that we would not—could not—close our doors. What would our scholars do? Atlanta Public Schools was a large and complex entity. We were small. We could weather this. We would carry on. There was no other option.

With signed paperwork in hand and a start date of July, Kimberly said her goodbyes, and I promised to be in touch soon.

Even with our proclamation that we would stay open, there was a growing sense of panic. My phone and email were blowing up. Partners. Staff. Parents. Everyone was scared and unsure. The medical community was clear only about the fact that we needed to prepare. It was a restless night for us all.

By the next morning, after discussions with partners, staff, parents, and the medical community, we made the decision to close our doors. Unlike the larger schools, though, we announced that we would reassess every two days.

With our decision made, the staff gathered to create learning packets and snack bags for our families. The parents came by throughout the day to pick up the packages. Then we went home and waited.

One day . . . one week . . . two weeks . . . COVID wasn't going away. Three weeks into our closure, we decided to purchase tablets for each of our scholars. We spent the week of spring break in masks and gloves personally delivering the tablets, more snack bags, and internet support options to each of our families. It was great to see them. Our little community had become so tight. Our abrupt separation had been jarring for us all—especially for our young scholars who counted on this constant in their lives. Our teachers collaborated and created online lessons to keep the scholars on track. Our social worker created opportunities for our parents to gather virtually. It wasn't enough, but we remained online for the remainder of the school year. There was just no other option.

CHAPTER FIFTEEN
Together and Apart

This is in the end the only kind of courage that is required of us: the courage to face the strangest, most unusual, most inexplicable experiences that can meet us.

—RAINER MARIA RILKE

It felt like the world had stopped. Most people that I knew were hunkered down trying to make the best of a bad situation, but the school still needed constant attention. Our families were shouldering a new ominous crisis on top of the daily crises that interrupted their journeys.

"What can I do?" asked Kimberly.

It was April, and she had called to check in. Was her job still secure? Did I need any help? I didn't even know what to tell her. Her official start date wasn't until July. There was a mountain to climb, and I had no idea how to begin, but I knew we needed her now more than ever. We were supposed to be moving into a new building. On top of our rent, we also needed new furniture and a few renovations. Then there was our increased payroll, but what if we weren't able to return to traditional school? What was our hope of raising funds for a fledgling program during a global pandemic?

"I've already fallen in love with this program," she said. "I can't wait to get started, and I have nothing going on right now. We just moved here, and we're just sitting here unpacking."

I didn't even realize how stressed and alone I felt until she reached out, but during the course of our conversation, I felt my shoulders release about six inches. My entire body breathed a sigh I didn't even know I was holding.

We decided that we would include each other in our COVID circle and made plans to meet at the new building the following week to collaborate.

Returning to our new space was like entering a dream once again. It was beautiful. Large glass garage doors separated the classrooms from the common areas. Brightly colored murals covered every wall. We would need to make some adjustments, but the space was more than I'd ever imagined.

Kimberly and I quickly became a dynamic duo. We were like old friends who'd been reunited. She was smart and funny and so experienced. Her default, much like mine, was to dream big and get stuff done. She had a vision that matched mine and even moved beyond. What a gift to have her by my side during this difficult time.

We borrowed a truck, and together, load by heavy load, we moved all the furniture from our space at St. Luke's to our new building. It was a Herculean effort. We moved desks and chairs, cabinets and tables, steel-lined filing cabinets and floor-to-ceiling organizers from one empty building to another. It was a stressful time, but we were unstoppable, and we laughed a lot.

We were up against incredible obstacles. It was hard and exhausting, but our little school continued even though COVID kept us apart. I shared monthly community newsletters filled with stories of our families and our online programs and our incredible new building. Our community responded through robust support for the program with regular donations.

"Do we need cubicles?" asked Kimberly one day as we were scrubbing baseboards and arranging furniture.

The open concept of our new space was a bonus but also had its drawbacks. Privacy would be difficult.

"I don't think they're in our budget," I said.

"I have a friend from out of town who has a friend here in Atlanta who's an office manager. The staff has decided to shift all their work to remote, and they said we can have their cubicle walls if we can pick them up."

Two days later, we'd found a moving company willing to pick up the cubicles from the empty office building and drop them off at our new building. That's how things worked between Kimberly and me: quickly and efficiently.

I'm not sure what I thought deconstructed cubicles were like. I think I'd pictured neat, easily moveable giant Lego pieces that snapped together. When the delivery was complete, what we had before us were hundreds of heavy panels in all shapes and sizes and even more screws, bolts, and connectors. I laughed and cried at the same time. We were stuck with these monstrosities, and for all the things that I can figure out, making sense out of this mess was not one of them. We consulted with people who were handier than we were. We dragged and measured. It was like a house of cards. One piece would stand just as another was collapsing. Of all the trials that we had overcome that long summer, the moment I was able to stand back and survey the rows of standing cubicles felt like the biggest win of all. I can raise money. I can build a school, but the cubicles almost took us down.

With the space taking shape, Kimberly and I began planning for the upcoming school year. One thing was very clear. Our scholars depended on us returning to in-person learning. They didn't have a consistent place or method of learning online and many of the parents didn't have the capacity to offer the support that four- and five-year-olds would require to learn online. The staff and board were supportive of the decision. The staff had been frustrated by the limitations of online teaching in our community. They were ready to be back in the classroom. Most of the families were thrilled with the decision to return to in-person school, but there was a handful of parents who were afraid. Our families were particularly vulnerable to the claws of COVID. Their living situations didn't always allow for appropriate distancing or quarantining. They lacked access to and confidence in medical care. Like all of us, for them, the consequences of contracting COVID were life-and-death.

This is why we started a small, private school. We could create a program to meet our scholars and their families where they were. Kimberly announced that she would continue an online option for any scholars who were uncomfortable returning in person. For all others, we would be back to in-person learning. Our new space offered plenty of room to distance. We were careful. We took as many precautions as possible, and we stayed in close communication with our families.

The decision paid off in so many important ways. First, we had only two cases of COVID during the entire school year, forcing us to revert to complete online learning for only one week during the year. Most importantly, while our scholars were still testing below their housed peers in other school systems, their test scores actually continued to rise during the year. Our program was working.

I was overjoyed at the success we were having, but it was also really hard. We needed to raise a lot of money, and that was hard during lockdown. With Kimberly focused on teaching our online scholars, the day-to-day operations and management of staff fell back to me. The stress levels were high. Both staff and scholars were living in constant fear of COVID. Every sniffle and cough sent the entire school into a panic. Even though the staff had requested to come back, the reality was heavy. So many of their colleagues in other schools weren't being asked to teach in person, and as time wore on, the requirement to keep showing up began to wear on them. It was so much more complicated than imagined. The staff was tired. The families were unsettled. Our program was offering more stability than the rest of life, but it was still so much to bear.

COVID heightened racial tension everywhere, and our school was no exception. We had worked hard to create a space that was culturally and racially sensitive and inclusive. All of our scholars and most of our staff identified as BIPOC.[9] Most of the board and staff leadership identified as white. Since the beginning, we had had frequent and honest conversations about how to recognize and honor both similarities and differences.

"I don't think it's appropriate for a white woman to be the face of this school," said our social worker one day.

She had requested a private meeting with me. She was a young, dynamic, black woman. She did an excellent job supporting our families through each crisis and mentoring the staff in best practices of handling trauma in the classroom. I was shocked by the statement. She and I had a close relationship. We had had lots of honest and open conversations. I learned so much from her about best practices of social work and about life as a black woman.

"Well—how do you think we should handle this?" I asked.

"I just feel like when you're in the community, you talk about the plight of the black community from the point of view of a privileged white woman who doesn't know what it feels like to be black or poor. There are always all these privileged white people walking through the building. They don't understand," she said.

Pre-COVID, there were a lot of rich white people in and out of the school. We needed their buy-in and support. Most of our funders wanted to better understand the inequities of our system. They wanted to be part of the solution. There were some who wanted to build a relationship beyond money, but there were others who just wanted to give from a distance. I worked hard to develop my voice in a way that would authentically honor the dignity of every one of our program, staff, and scholars.

"I try really hard to use my privilege to open doors for our scholars. I count on the input of our entire staff to help me speak your story through my story," I said.

Our conversation continued. I'm sure I misspoke along the way, but my intentions were good. We ended the meeting with a stronger relationship and a greater respect for each other and the challenges we both faced.

CHAPTER SIXTEEN
Privilege and Purpose

When we identify where our privilege intersects
with somebody else's oppression, we'll find our
opportunities to make real change.

—IJEOMA OLUO

I was raised in a landscape of wealth and manners and Southern hospitality, but I was also always a little rebellious. By most anyone's standards, I was an exemplary child. I had nice friends. Adults loved me. I earned good grades and was involved at church. My problem or gift was that I always pushed against what was expected of me. I knew there must be a bigger world outside of the safe haven of my childhood, and I wanted to experience it.

"Why is what we have here for you not enough?" my parents would ask in frustration and confusion.

And I could never answer them. I only knew that there was something more that I was missing in our tiny bubble.

Choosing to attend college seven hours from my hometown was my first big step. At the time, I thought I was being tremendously bold and broad-minded, but as much as I loved my school and as wonderful of an experience as I had during those four years, it was really just a baby step. I was so sheltered and so naïve that I didn't even realize what it meant to spread my wings. You don't know what you don't know, and I didn't have a clue how the world really worked. I had yet to discover the breadth and depth of the world. I thought my baby steps were giant leaps.

I look back now and laugh (and cringe) at my ignorance. My school was far away, but it was a smallish, private, competitive, liberal arts university with a student body whose majority looked and acted and viewed the world much like I did. Yes, I was far from home, and yes, to my parents, I was rebelling and breaking free, but in truth, the vast expanse of diversity and the inequity of opportunities that defined our world remained unseen to me.

My grandmother (who would have preferred I call her by her first name—"Miss Katherine"—but settled for the moniker of "Grandmother") was always dismissive and likely disappointed with my desires to break out of the "way we always do things." It frustrated her that I didn't go to the "right" college or pledge the "right" sorority or set my sights on finding a husband ASAP. She considered my choices to be a personal affront to my heritage. Yet, on the day I graduated from college, she pulled me aside, and in the corner of the large reception room, she presented me with a small, perfectly wrapped package.

"Thank you, Grandmother," I said as I turned around to rejoin my friends and the celebration.

"Will you open it now?" she asked.

I stopped mid exit and returned my attention to the gift. Inside the small box, I found a gold charm bracelet with eight intricate charms: a cruise ship, a pair of Dutch clogs, a gold crown, a rail car, a German cuckoo clock, a beer stein, an Italian wine vessel, and the Eiffel Tower. She explained that she had created the bracelet from charms she collected throughout her trip to Europe via an Atlantic Ocean crossing.

"This is really pretty, Grandmother. Thanks," I said, already turning back to my friends and the party.

Then, in a moment that would forever change my relationship with Grandmother, she said, "I want you to have this because you are my grandchild who's going to see the world. You are my grandchild who's going to change the world."

Then she kissed me on the head and told me to go and celebrate. In that moment, I saw a part of Grandmother that had remained elusive to me for my entire life. I suddenly felt more confident in my desire to do bold, brave things, to forge new paths, and to try to figure out what the world was really all about. I was still naïve and sheltered and ignorant, but I felt validated in my dreams.

As I have experienced a greater tapestry of life, I have continued to struggle with the privilege and "breeding" of my formative years. It winds its way through all that I am and all that I have become. The world is hurting. The systems into which so many people are born are unfair. It's taken me decades to begin to understand that I can't remove the threads of my formation, but I can use them as the gifts that they are. Grandmother recognized my longing to be part of the larger world. I believe each of our calls is to intertwine all of who we are and all of who we are becoming in a way that allows us to offer the most beauty, hope, and love to the greater tapestry of the world. In the words of Parker Palmer, we "must listen to [our] lives and try to understand what [they are] truly about."[10]

Yet I still find it difficult to reconcile my two worlds. As a privileged white woman, I have felt guilty for claiming struggles. I have felt unworthy to lift up my story. What do I have to complain about? Who cares what I have to say? For years, I privately journaled my internal voices and frustrations while publicly keeping my polished persona intact. I strived to use every ounce of my privilege to give voice to those whose voices are too often silenced. My recompense, as I saw it, for being privileged was to bury my own story in order to stand in quiet solidarity with those who truly had reason to feel hurt. My story, in my mind, was inconsequential to the needs of the world. It has taken a long time, but I now see that our stories are all connected. We're all connected. Our invitation is to listen to each story and identify the places where we allow one another to grow. Sadly, I don't think our world is always ready for that. Instead, our stories become our armor or our albatross. We use them to divide rather than unite. We use them to protect rather than embrace.

One of my many privileges and a big part of my story was the opportunity to stay home with my children, but it definitely came at a cost. The overwhelming message to so many women is that staying at home is repressive or old-fashioned. Women (including myself) who identify as Gen X are especially prone to this struggle. In her book, *Why We Can't Sleep*, Ada Calhoun explains that our mothers and the generation of women before them had very limited opportunities. They worked diligently to break the glass ceiling, pushing through laws like Title IX that gave girls equal access to athletic and academic opportunities. The generation of women before Gen X lit a torch, which they passed down to their daughters with the expectation that they would seize their newly minted opportunity to have it all, but we often find the ask to be too big. We were supposed to be full-time mothers and full-time CEOs which, as Calhoun explains, is why so many of us can't sleep.[11] Choosing to give up a professional career to be a full-time, stay-at-home mother is often seen as an affront to the women who worked so hard to make our dreams a reality. Someone once even asked me why I bothered to go to college if I was going to stay home with my children.

I admit that on my worst days, I sometimes wonder the same, but the choice to stay home was made in partnership with my husband. We decided it was the best choice for our family, and we were in a position to be able to make it happen. I didn't choose to stay home with my children full-time because there were no other options. I had a great career. I loved my job, and I could choose my path. It took a long time, but seeing my life this way helped me to understand that, contrary to popular opinion, you can be a feminist and a stay-at-home mom. The power of womanhood comes from working to write a story that is right for you and respecting and supporting other women in their stories. My journey to build The Ansley School was, in many ways, not only a reflection of my hopes and dreams for children but also for their moms. In the end, it's all about understanding the worth of your own story.

But, again, this way of thinking came only after years of reflecting and growing. And this way of thinking still only works on my best days. On my worst days, I fall victim to the narrative that I'm not smart enough or professional enough. On my worst days, I'm the naïve imposter who thought she could change the system with a new way of thinking. On my worst days, I'm ashamed of my privilege and what I have or have not done with it. For the most part, our culture supports this narrative. I didn't have a lucrative, high-paying, corporate job. I was in the work force full-time for only six years before I jumped off the corporate ladder to stay home with my children.

Looking back, this perspective—both personal and societal—was the one that undermined me and my ability to continue to lead the school that I created. Instead of trusting in myself, I listened to those who had more corporate experience, more business experience, more degrees, and more stories of loss. I didn't have the confidence in myself to believe a different narrative—ironically, a narrative that was successfully living out in real time. The school was growing and blossoming. The funding was reliable. I should have trusted myself or at least understood that the success that was happening all around me was of my doing and my ability. A little too late, I realized that—title or no title, salary or no salary, corporate experience or no corporate experience— I knew what I was doing. My story was worth living out. I should have believed in myself.

CHAPTER SEVENTEEN
Grief Compounded

Maybe death isn't darkness after all,
but so much light wrapping itself around us.

—MARY OLIVER

It was just past dawn when we pulled out of my sister's neighborhood. A light rain fell. The kind of rain that makes the windshield wipers necessary but annoying. Today, though, in the weight of the silence, their rhythmic whir and scrape were a calming distraction.

It was December of 2020, deep in the middle of the COVID lockdown. My sister and I had received the call just an hour earlier.

"Your father doesn't have much time," said the kind nurse. "If you come now, I can let you in to see him."

Our dad had been living in a skilled nursing facility since his "catastrophic" stroke during our mom's funeral just over one year ago. It had been a gut-wrenching decision to make, but we didn't see any other options. The facility we chose was in Huntsville, Alabama, where our other sister lived with her family. Until recently, Dad had been thriving beyond expectation in his new home. The staff loved him and treated him with respect and loving care. Although his dementia was severe and his mobility limited, the rest of his health had significantly improved since moving into the facility. He was off most of his medication, and he seemed content. It was still hard to see our dad, who had been a brilliant physician, theologian, and academic, in a state of such decline, but the fact that he was at peace and cheerful was so comforting.

My Huntsville sister visited Dad every day, and my Atlanta sister and I came up separately one Saturday each month. It was always good for my soul to spend time with my dad. Although his confusion could be unsettling, the time we spent together playing bingo in the activity room with his friends, sharing a meal, or just sitting side by side watching television was a gift. His sense of humor and kind demeanor never wavered.

My sisters and I were also spending time making trips to Birmingham to clean out our parents' house and make arrangements to sell it. It was exhausting and emotional work. I was so glad to have my sisters by my side as we walked this difficult path.

Then came COVID and the end of our visits. Dad was not well enough to have a conversation on the phone, so we kept up with him through sweet notes and updates from the nursing staff. Our Huntsville sister stood below Dad's third floor window each day and waved. The staff would help him look out the window. We weren't sure if he understood who she was or what she was doing from so far below, but she was there every day. Summer passed, then Thanksgiving. There seemed to be no end in sight to this new normal, but still, Dad seemed happy and at peace.

In December, he contracted COVID. He should have died when Mom died. He wanted to die when Mom died, yet he kept on living. So, when COVID caught up with him, we opted not to take any lifesaving measures. The staff moved him to the COVID floor of the facility and kept him comfortable. Early on the morning of December 12, I got the call we had been expecting and dreading.

Our ride to Huntsville was quiet. The cold rain continued to fall even as the sun rose higher in the sky. The nurse called us several times along the way asking how close we were. Dad was comfortable, but time was running short.

It was a gift that we were even allowed to be with him. If he had been in a hospital, this wouldn't have been possible, but still, significant precautions were required. There was no vaccine yet, so we were knowingly exposing ourselves to a deadly virus that we knew very little about. One at a time, we suited up in our hazmat gear—triple masks, full body suit and head covering—and we took turns by his bed. I went last. I was concerned he wouldn't recognize me. It had been months since we had seen him. His dementia had increased. I was dressed like an alien, and he was so near the end.

"Dad," I said when I entered his room, "it's Kate. I love you."

He grunted and nodded and squeezed my hand. My dad and I had always been connected by our love of church and theology. So, as I made myself comfortable on the edge of his bed, I began to sing.

"Amazing grace, how sweet the sound," I sang in a shaky voice.

His eyes opened and closed. The oxygen machine whirred. His breathing was erratic, so I just kept singing. After a few hymns, we prayed, and then sat in silence for a long moment.

"God is with you, Dad," I finally said through my tears. "God is saying, 'Well done my faithful servant. Well done, my beloved.' Your girls are going to be alright. Just rest."

My dad was stubborn and would protect his girls at all costs. Just as I knew in my gut that he had been holding on the previous year just to make sure we would be OK, I also knew in my gut that he wouldn't die while I was by his side. But I didn't want him to be alone, so I asked the nurse to sit with him and left the room. He died within five minutes. The nurse told me that he cried out in a loud voice then looked up over her shoulder, smiled, and died.

My sisters and I sat in silence for a long time. We were orphans. As odd as that might sound, that's what I kept saying to myself. But we were also at peace knowing that Dad's final moment had warranted a smile, and he and Mom were finally back together again.

We exited the parking lot of the facility and went directly to the nearest drug store where we bought every type of sanitizer we could find. Aerosol, gel, and cream for clothing, skin, and air. We changed our clothes and doused ourselves with cleaning fluids. I even sprayed Lysol in our hair. COVID was a large, threatening beast, and we wanted no part of it.

The car ride home was quiet. The rain had picked up its pace and power. I couldn't help but think that the earth was mourning with us. Dad had been clear in life that he never wanted to be mourned. He wanted to be celebrated. His dream was for his remains to be driven around the town in a large hearse with hymns blaring out of loudspeakers. He envisioned neighbors and friends and colleagues lining the streets to say goodbye.

Instead, COVID restrictions would allow only immediate family to gather. So, we designed a COVID-safe parade to celebrate Dad's life. The obituary shared details of the livestream and invited the community to drive through the church parking lot immediately following the service to pay their respects from a socially safe distance.

The day of the service was cold and dreary. We had sold our parents' house, so we had to stay in a hotel. It felt strange being in our hometown with no home. Our anchors were gone. Now, we were each other's anchor, and we were holding on tightly as we walked down the long aisle to celebrate our dad. The sanctuary of my childhood church had always been a place of refuge for me. When our family was at church on Sundays, I felt like we were the best version of ourselves. The sanctuary was a place of love and joy and so many milestones: my baptism, my confirmation, my sending forth to college, my wedding, the weddings of my sisters and so many of my friends, and now the funerals of both of my parents. With a capacity of nine hundred, the large space felt empty with only our immediate family to fill the pews, but this space had never let me down. I always felt a sense of love and support. This was the closest thing to home that I had left in my hometown, and I couldn't imagine celebrating my dad anywhere else.

We were solemn as we exited the sanctuary following the service. As we walked downstairs and toward the parking lot, we noticed a line of cars waiting at the drop-off. Dad's parade was underway. For as far as I could see, cars lined the street. One by one, they began moving past the door—honking, waving, blowing kisses, and tossing notes and flowers for us to collect. For almost two hours, we waved and cried and watched as our dad's parade rolled by. He would've been so happy. The thought made me happy, but I was still so very sad. I was now grieving both of my parents, and the weight of running the school pressed in all around me.

—

I returned to Atlanta and to the school just a few days following the service. While I was away, the stress of the day-to-day of the school had continued to grow. The staff was tired. The scholars and families were tired. It felt like this new way of being might never end.

Kimberly and I decided to reach out to our community partner in mental health care. They'd been crucial in our ability to understand trauma care for both our scholars and our staff. Together, we had put several safety nets in place for the staff. Secondary trauma and compassion fatigue are real threats to anyone working with a traumatized population. During this time, we requested help in hosting a facilitated listening session with the staff.

We gathered with the staff in the library at 4 p.m. The scholars were gone for the day, and the building was quiet. The exhaustion of everyone was palpable. It had been a long day and a long year.

The facilitator invited each of us to find a chair in the circle she'd constructed. On the board were several questions: "What is overwhelming you right now?" "What support do you need?" "What is going well?" "What is your vision for the remainder of the school year?" One by one, we were asked to share our responses with the group.

The answers were not surprising. Everyone felt stressed and overworked. Everyone felt frustrated and under-appreciated. Everyone wanted the scholars to thrive but admitted that they weren't sure they could do what it takes to keep the school going. We were all feeling the same thing.

Maybe it was a generational thing. Maybe it was a personality thing, but there was a clear division in how each of us thought the problem should be handled. Kimberly and I were ready to put our heads down and get the work done. The staff proposed a break. I just didn't see any way that would work. We couldn't afford substitutes, and our scholars couldn't afford disruption in their schedules. The conversation was calm and caring. It was difficult but respectful. We were a team. We just couldn't find a way forward. Christmas break was right around the corner. We hoped that we'd all find some rest and renewal over the break.

CHAPTER EIGHTEEN
Deep Listening

Before I can tell my life what I want to do with it, I must listen to my life telling me who I am.

—PARKER PALMER

The renewal experienced over Christmas break was short-lived. COVID was wearing on everyone. The break simply reminded the staff of all the people who weren't required to show up in person for their work. It felt unfair. It was unfair, but we had no solution. We had to keep going. The scholars and their families needed us.

The perfect storm was building. Looking back, we could all feel it coming, but none of us was prepared for the deluge. COVID continued to assault our world. The brutal murders of black men and women including Ahmaud Arbery, Breonna Taylor, and George Floyd had thrown our entire country into a state of deep stress and division. Racial tensions were high. Generational divides were growing. The world was on tilt, bracing for a fall and hoping for a miracle.

Inside the school, things weren't much better. Serving families in crisis and trauma can be soul-crushing. Showing up day after day when so many were tucked safely away in their homes was frustrating. None of us could find sufficient ways to care for ourselves. I wanted to support the staff, but I couldn't figure out how. As the tension in the world continued to bear down on our already stressed school, the powerful storm grew stronger, and we struggled to find our way.

Every day was difficult, but still we persevered. We all loved the program and the scholars, and we loved each other. We had been together for a long time and had built this school together. We just had to figure out how to weather the storm.

I was at my desk late one day waiting with a child whose mother was stuck on the subway. As we sat side by side coloring and chatting, the phone rang. It was a number I didn't recognize, but I assumed it was about the child.

"This is Kate," I answered.

"Hi, Kate," said the man on the other end of the line. "We haven't met, but I've been following your school for some time. My wife and I are so impressed by what you're doing. We've just received some family money and would like to make a transformational gift to the school."

A "transformational gift," he had said. We needed something transformational.

Since COVID had made hosting community tours of our program and new space an impossibility, Kimberly and I had hosted a video tour and a live question-and-answer session online for the community. This couple had attended the virtual event and wanted to make a difference. We scheduled a Zoom meeting for the following week. When I disconnected the call and looked at my little friend, so sweet and innocent, sitting next to me swinging her legs while drawing a tree on her paper, I felt more at peace than I had in a long time.

The Zoom meeting went well. After presenting our budget and our hopes and dreams for the program, the couple asked several questions. Then, I'd shared a list of sponsorship opportunities that I'd prepared. The list included ideas such as sponsoring an individual child or sponsoring our nutrition program. Several of the options had sounded interesting to them, but none of them really resonated.

"We want to do something outside the box," they said. "Sponsoring a child or a lunch program is great, but we want to sponsor something that you feel is indispensable and maybe not sexy to another funder."

I thought for a minute, and then it hit me.

"This organization is a little different because we're a school, but we're also a nonprofit," I said. "This means we need two leaders: a principal to build and run an academic institution and a president to build and run a two-million-dollar nonprofit. Right now, I'm serving as president for no salary. I would love to find funding for this position, so we could staff it officially," I explained.

"Now that's the kind of thing that we were thinking of," they exclaimed. "What if we thought about funding the position of president for five years?"

What a gift. This was the best news I'd heard in so long. Once things were settled and the world was back to normal, we could hire someone to take my staff role, and I could return to the board of directors. I thanked them wholeheartedly, and we arranged a follow-up for the next week.

"You won't believe this," I excitedly told an executive committee member the next day. "A funder has offered to fund the president salary for the next five years!"

"That is very generous, but you can't accept it. We're still not sure we have the right organizational structure. We may not actually need a president going forward."

I was stunned. I was the one there every day. The organizational structure may need some tweaks, but running a school and raising two million dollars would take more than one leader.

"Ask them to fund something else," said my colleague.

"We went through everything. This is what they want to do. I think it's an amazing gift," I said.

"You can't take it if that is what it's for."

My heart sank. That evening, my husband and I had a long and emotional conversation. I was overwhelmed. Like the rest of the staff, I felt unsupported. I felt abandoned by the board. I was there every day dealing with everything. It was slowly killing me, but this program was my heart.

"I don't know if I can do this," I said to my husband through tears, "but I also don't know how not to do it."

I've never felt so conflicted and helpless. I truly did not know how to move forward.

———

Parker Palmer is a sociologist and writer whose work has always inspired me. As a Quaker, he draws frequently from the tradition. It's through his work that I first learned of Clearness Committees. Dating back to the 1600s, Clearness Committees are groups of three to five people who gather to support a person who is discerning a path or a call. The goal of the Clearness Committee is not to fix the situation but to remove "interference so that they can discover their own wisdom from inside out." The process spoke to my soul. The interference was unrelenting, and I needed to get unstuck.[12]

I reached out to three dear friends. One was connected to the school and the other two were not. They all really knew me. None of them were familiar with the process of a Clearness Committee, but all were willing to gather with me.

I sent them information on the process and some background information describing my dilemma. We agreed to meet one evening via Zoom. Their role was to ask me deep questions. My role was only to answer what they asked.

"How do you feel right now?" one of my friends asked at the start of our virtual gathering.

"I feel exhausted and frustrated and hopeless, but I love the kids and the program," I answered.

"I didn't ask you if you loved the kids. I only asked how you felt right now," said my friend.

She had clearly read the information I sent her. These women weren't going to let me off the hook easily. Over the next hour, my committee asked deep and meaningful questions. When our time ended, I felt loved and supported, but I wanted a way forward, and still I felt conflicted and helpless.

Looking back, I understand the gift and the turning point of that moment. It was never supposed to be a quick fix. I knew that from the start—at least in my mind. It was supposed to help me quiet the noise and trust myself so I could better hear what God was calling me to do next. I know this takes time. I know slowing down and listening requires time and space, but I couldn't convince myself to lean into the process. I really wanted a concrete answer on what to *do* next.

Chaos continued to hold my attention. It was so pushy and loud. I just thought that if I could tackle one crisis at a time, a sustainable path would eventually emerge. To the outside world, I was a rock star. The school was growing. The money was coming in. The scholars were thriving even in the tumultuous climate. Chaos is quick and reactive. It is energizing but unsustainable. Calm is slow and quiet. It's not glamorous, but it is true and lasting. Calm was also too scary for me to embrace. It felt too much like losing control. So, I just stayed on the treadmill hoping for a breakthrough.

In the spring of 2021, we hosted an in-person strategic planning session. For most of the board members, this was their first opportunity to see our amazing new space. Spirits were high. Everyone loved the space and was excited to dream and strategize. After the tour, we turned the meeting over to the planning firm we had hired to facilitate.

"We will use the colorful post-it notes in front of each of you to begin a SWOT analysis of the program. Strengths on pink. Weaknesses on yellow. Opportunities on blue. Threats on purple," instructed our facilitator.

The room became quiet as everyone recorded their thoughts. Pens scribbled on paper, and the facilitators used tape to attach two posters to opposite walls. They read, "Board" and "Staff."

"As you finish," said the facilitator, "place each of your post-it notes under the most fitting poster. Is the staff responsible for this or the board?"

There was buzzing and bustling in the large room as we each jockeyed our way to the different walls. When all were displayed, we stood back and studied the lists. There was one—not written by me—on the designated "threat" post-it that immediately caught my eye. It simply said, "Kate gets hit by a bus."

"Who wrote that?" I asked, both jokingly and relieved at the recognition of the bigger issue.

"I did," responded a board member. "We hope you don't actually get hit by a bus, but if you did, we would be sunk."

I was so relieved. We were going to find a way through. Maybe they did have my back. My hopes were suspended, though, as we finished the day without another mention of the purple post-it note that held my name.

CHAPTER NINETEEN
Falling Hard

One of the main tasks of theology is to find words that do not divide but unite, that do not create conflict but unity, that do not hurt but heal.

–HENRI NOUWEN

It was 4 p.m. on a Wednesday. The scholars had left for the day, and the teachers were gathering for their regular midweek check-ins. I had been in outside meetings all day, but I could tell when I entered the room that something had happened. There was a tension and an energy that was different from just a regular day. I took my seat as the meeting began.

A teacher was out sick that day, so there had been a substitute in one of the classrooms. Over the years, we'd tried different solutions to cover teacher absences, but none had worked well. Our school wasn't a mainstream school. Our scholars needed special support, and our classroom management techniques were specifically designed to provide that support. Introducing a short-term person into the classroom system was always a delicate balance.

Today, one of our scholars had used a racial slur to address the substitute teacher. Some of our scholars used rough language. It was a side effect of growing up on the streets. We didn't want to be judgmental of the way anyone spoke, but we worked hard at helping our scholars, families, and staff understand that not all ways of speaking are appropriate in all situations. Words we might use at home or with a group of our peers were not always appropriate to say at school or in the workplace.

Language differs across culture and family and setting. All people, but truthfully, mostly those from minority populations, must use shifts of language to fit in and be accepted in the majority system. I learned to shift the way I speak subconsciously as my family modelled it for me. (The technical term for this skill is "code-switching.")[13] Expressions as basic as saying, "I have to pee" when I'm at home or when I'm hanging out with my friends but knowing that when I'm in a more formal setting, I should say, "I need to use the restroom" are important skills that help me more successfully navigate in the world. Generational poverty, especially within marginalized communities, can rob children of the opportunity to build this important skill. In most cases, the parents don't model the skill because they never had the chance to learn it themselves.

As I settled in my seat on that Wednesday afternoon, one of the staff began describing the incident. The substitute had been upset and angry. She had left the classroom and the building prior to the end of the day. I would need to follow up with the agency immediately after this meeting. We would also need to make a plan to contact the scholar and his family. This was bad. It was disheartening, but it wasn't completely surprising. This, again, is why we began this school. Our children and families lived on the margins and needed the special community to guide and support them as they gathered the tools to be in the world in a sustainable way. I was taking notes and privately brainstorming how to best handle the situation as the conversation continued.

"What did he call her?" a staff member asked.

"He called her the n-word," she replied, and used the *actual* word.

My head bolted upright. I was not prepared for this. This word held so much anger and hatred. I couldn't believe that it had been uttered in its entirety in our meeting. It was very concerning that a child had spoken it, but even more shocking to hear it in this context. I could feel heaviness rising in my chest. I scanned the room, looking for others' reaction to the word. No one had missed a beat. The meeting was continuing as if this were just one of the many challenges the staff faced each week.

"I think we need to have some sort of special training for our substitutes before they're thrown into the classroom," someone was saying.

The conversation continued. Both the student and the substitute were black. No one was sure why the student had used the word. Was he testing it or repeating something he had heard someone say? We had a lot to untangle, but to my relief, the utterance of the word in this meeting didn't seem to bring about the same punch-in-the-gut feeling for anyone but me. I decided not to make a big deal of it in the meeting but to pull the staff person aside and let them know that it was inappropriate to ever use that word—even to repeat it—in our building.

The rest of the meeting was productive. Our staff was at its best when we were working together to get through a crisis. We continued to brainstorm and come up with new best practices.

The staff person who uttered the word was apologetic when I approached her separately the next day.

"I was just repeating what he said, but I thought a lot about it last night, and I agree that the word doesn't have a place in our school," she said. "It was a bad decision, and I'm really sorry."

We agreed that it was an innocent mistake, but one that could never happen again. It was just one more challenge in a school filled with challenges, or at least, that is what I thought at the time.

⸺

I was at home cooking spaghetti for my family when the text came through. It was from a board member. It read,

Check your email.

Maybe we had been awarded a new grant, I thought. I grabbed my phone and opened my email while continuing to stir the marinara sauce on the stove top. I scrolled my inbox: requests to partner, a report of bounced emails from our newsletter marketing platform, PTO requests from staff, and then I saw it—a letter to the board of directors from a staff person. She was reporting the use of a racial slur in a staff meeting by another staff person. Her letter stated that she had been so traumatized by the utterance of the word that she felt uncomfortable at work. I couldn't breathe.

She and I had always been close. In the wake of the George Floyd killing, she had asked me to put out a statement on behalf of the school. I had told her that I didn't think anyone cared what a middle-aged white woman had to say on the subject. She disagreed, so I asked her to help me draft something. Together, she and I had come up with a succinct yet powerful statement that we posted on the school Instagram page. She was young, but so wise, and I appreciated her support and candor.

Several weeks after the use of the slur in our meeting, she had come to me to say that it had upset her. I confessed that it had upset me, as well.

"What are you going to do about it?" she asked.

I explained that I had spoken to the staff member responsible and the parents of the young boy, but I also tried to explain to her that there was a difference between actively using the slur (which the young boy had done) and passively using it (as the staff person had done). I apologized and assured her that we were focused on building a safe and healthy workplace. I thought all was well, but as the pressures of our world continued to bear down, our fears sat right at the surface of everything. The racial tension and violence that was playing out on our streets affected each of us and unsettled our fragile equilibrium.

When I saw her email to the board that early spring evening, I knew that a door had been opened that could never be closed.

The board, who had, for the most part, been happy to sit in the background, jumped into action. They were scared and shocked. They brought in attorneys to do a formal investigation.

"I didn't mean for all this to happen," said the staff person who had written the letter. "I just wanted the board to get more involved."

"I'm so sorry you were upset. I appreciate everything you do. We're all so tired. This has been a really long year," I told her as we sat in the school lobby.

There was really nothing more to say. The attorneys were interviewing every person on staff, one by one. It was disruptive and stressful. The teachers complained about the time they had to be away from class or stay after work hours. The whole thing was a mess, and Kimberly and I truly thought it would quickly blow over. We were wrong.

I never read the attorneys' final report, but the board stated that there were some damning accusations. They assured me that neither they nor the attorneys thought I had done anything wrong, but they wondered aloud how I could have let this happen on my watch.

"We know you didn't do or say anything inappropriate," said a board member to me on a call following the investigation. "It's just that you were in charge. You were there. Did you not see this coming?"

I later learned that most of the accusations came from one teacher—not the one who had written to the board. We had recently discovered that she had lied about her credentials on her résumé. She wasn't performing well in the classroom, and her contract wasn't going to be renewed for the following year. She had told the attorneys that the leadership was creating a culturally insensitive environment. She had worn slippers to work one day, and I had commented that her shoes were not appropriate for work. Neither were leggings or T-shirts with messaging or jeans with holes. All this was in our handbook, but to her, this was culturally motivated insensitivity. All the incidents she described in the report lacked important context.

In the end, the board opted to renew her contract. Kimberly and I argued, but they stood firm. It wasn't right. She wasn't qualified, but now the board felt stuck.

"Leave it alone, Kate" they told me as I tried to change their decision.

After the investigation, the board took over daily operations of the school. Their trust in me was damaged, and truthfully, my trust in them was damaged, as well. They told me that the new role they were offering me was exactly what

I had been asking for. On the surface, it *was* what I had been asking for—the opportunity to just be out in the community raising funds and awareness. The problem was that no one was stepping in to pick up all the other things that I had been doing to keep the school running every day. After the formal investigation, several staff, including Kimberly, had left the school. Some were asked to leave, and others just moved on. The staff that remained was not only a mere shadow of its former self, but also traumatized and overwhelmed.

The board was urgently seeking a new head of school, but during this time, someone needed to be doing the work. I panicked as I continued to hear about things falling through the cracks. The rent had to be paid. The payroll had to be approved, and all the school pets needed daily care and feeding, but I felt helpless and conflicted. The whole situation seemed like a giant misunderstanding, but the board continued to hold firm in their position. They needed a scapegoat to distance themselves from it all. I guess that was me.

During the investigation, the board had moved to closed-door meetings. Once the reports were in, they opted to remain in closed sessions. I was invited to make reports but never to stay. During one Zoom meeting, I asked if I could stay on and just listen.

"I won't say anything," I said. "I just want to hear what is happening in the day-to-day. It's really important for fundraising."

An awkward pause followed, and then the response came. "No. It's really not appropriate for you to be here."

And with that, the screen went blank. If you have never been kicked off a Zoom meeting, I can tell you that it's a humiliating experience. Tears burned my eyes as I sat in my kitchen staring at the blank screen. What was I going to do? The situation was untenable.

When the new head of school came on board, I spent a couple of months sharing information and helping her get up to speed while I continued to focus on fundraising in the community, but there was a tension and a disconnect. Many on the board were longtime friends of mine who had joined the group when I first shared my vision. We had walked this groundbreaking path as a team. It had been rough at times, but we had always been confident that we were building something beautiful together. And yet now, it looked like our visions were diverging. We didn't trust one another. We weren't working as a team. The division was stressful and confusing. We were doing a dance that was unsustainable for any of us.

"What about the strategic plan?" I asked one day during my report to the board.

We had created that beautiful plan for growth just a few months prior. It was an important road map for our future. Sharing the plan and the progress were important keys to raising funds.

"We're volunteers," said one board member. "We don't have time to take care of all those things."

"But the funders will want to see our progress," I argued. "I can't raise funds without insight into what's happening on the ground at the school and a solid plan for growth."

My words fell on deaf ears. They were not in a place to think about growth. They had gone into survival mode, and I wasn't sure I could support that vision in the community.

CHAPTER TWENTY
With Integrity and Grace

*I do not at all understand the mystery of grace—
only that it meets us where we are but does not
leave us where it found us.*

–ANNE LAMOTT

I'm not certain what actually happened. I can't put my finger on a specific moment or event. My exit from the school was both my choice and not my choice. It was clear that the board wanted to keep me at arm's length. In their view, I had let something really destructive happen on my watch, and they were afraid to let me be too close to the daily operations. But it also felt like they were scared to completely push me out. I was frustrated to have people making sweeping decisions about what happened without really being there. The exact details were so tender and nuanced.

Over the years, I have tried again and again to make sense of what unfolded—to explain how it happened, to understand my role in the mess. The story I carry is my story from my perspective. Borrowing a sentiment from of one of my greatest inspirations, Father Richard Rohr, my point of view is nothing more than one view from one point.[14] There is so much I still don't proclaim to know or understand, but here is what I do know:

I know that I loved that school with a passion so powerful that it encompassed my entire being.

I know that at times, I probably hung on too tightly.

I know that giving up my seat on the board of directors was the beginning of the end for me.

I know that I let people on the board convince me that they were wiser and more experienced than I—that their opinions were more educated than mine.

I know that I should have trusted my own ability and insights.

I know that the racial tension in the world affected the strength and courage of both the board and the staff.

I know that I loved and respected each and every young scholar and parent who entered our doors.

I know that I did a really good job of building, running, sustaining, and growing a program that was bigger than any of us.

I know that it took more courage and strength to walk away than to stay.

I know that I left with integrity and grace.

CHAPTER TWENTY-ONE

Stillness

*When you come out of the storm you won't be
the same person who walked in.
That's what the storm's all about.*

–HARUKI MURAKAMI

The photograph still hangs on my magnet board. Crossed ankles, bare feet, outstretched legs resting on a small red table. In the background, a view of the lake—still, expansive, and peaceful. It was a sunny day, and I felt, for the first time in longer than I could remember, a sense of joy. It wasn't the energetic driving joy brought on by success and accomplishment. It was a deep and peaceful joy. It didn't make me tired. It made me satisfied.

It was June of 2021. That morning, I had met with the executive committee of the board to let them know that I would be stepping away from the school. The meeting was over Zoom and very short.

My husband and I had arrived at the lake the previous night. I hoped the distance would give me some space. I had requested this meeting with the executive committee days earlier and had carefully planned what I would say. I logged onto the meeting link a couple minutes early and tried to collect my thoughts. One by one, the other members of the executive committee popped up in their tiny boxes. When all were on, I took a deep breath and began.

"Building this school has been one of the greatest joys of my life. I am so proud of the program we have created, but it's time for me to step away," I said.

My voice sounded much stronger than I felt. My whole body was trembling. I don't think I had slept for one minute the previous night. My mind was racing. I'd practiced my speech over and over. I had analyzed and reanalyzed my decision. For once, I had decided to trust myself. This decision had not been made swiftly or carelessly.

Until recently, leaving the school had been unthinkable. The idea of The Ansley School going on without me made me physically ill. I couldn't even bear to imagine a world in which the program would exist without my involvement. I had given it every piece of me. But here we were. I had no other option.

I briefly expressed my concern that my vision for the school was no longer shared by the board. I didn't feel comfortable asking people to give money to an organization that I had lost trust in.

A stunned group of directors stared at me through the computer screen. No one said a word. The silence seemed to last an eternity. For a moment, I wondered if my connection had frozen. Then someone coughed.

"OK," I finally said, breaking the silence. "Well, I'm sure you all have a lot to talk about, so I'll drop off."

"Thank you, Kate," came a voice, and the screen went blank.

As I stared at the blank screen, I felt nothing. There was a tap at the door, and my husband appeared.

"It's done," I said.

He gave me a long hug, and while still holding me close he whispered, "You handled this in the only way possible. There was no other choice you could've made."

A few minutes later, I was alone, sitting on the dock by the lake with my feet propped up. As I stared at the water, I realized that I had nothing to do. I had nowhere to be. I didn't need to check my phone or my email. My children would be arriving for the weekend later that evening. For the next eight hours, there was absolutely nothing I had to do. When was the last time that had been my reality? For the moment, I could just be.

My thoughts were interrupted by my husband's cheerful voice.

"Want to take a ride in the kayak? I'm going to do some fishing."

"Absolutely." I exclaimed.

The two of us boarded the pedal fishing kayak that I had given him several Christmases ago and headed out into the open water. The sun felt warm on my back. There was a soft breeze blowing. I closed my eyes, and I felt completely free.

"I have nothing to do," I said as I leaned back and turned my face to the sun.

"I know," he said. "Just remember this feeling."

I think, in the back of my mind, I assumed this would all fix itself. My time away would be a reset for us all. The dust would settle. The school would adjust to stand on its own, and I would end up back on the board of directors. As the days and weeks and months passed, though, reality began to set in. After several failed attempts to find a way for me to stay connected, the door slammed shut. Too many things were said. Too many relationships were ruptured. Too much trust was lost. I was deeply wounded, and I feared the relationship was irrevocable.

"I'm afraid you are going to run out of time to have any influence at the school," said a friend who was still serving on the board.

We were sitting at an outdoor café having a glass of wine.

"There is nothing more I can do," I said.

I was destroyed. The peace and calm I had felt on that glorious day on the lake was quickly replaced with deep grief and loneliness. I missed the children and their families so much. I truly believed in what we had built. I gave my heart and soul to the program, and now I found myself driving to a grocery store miles away from my neighborhood so I wouldn't risk running into anyone on the board. Everywhere I went, people asked me how the school was going, and I didn't know what to say. The encounters continued to make me physically ill.

The empty time stretched out before me like a deep cavern of nothing. I had neglected my friendships and hobbies for so long while I was working at the school. Life had continued to move along, and now, I couldn't find a place to fit. I was so bored. I was so lonely. I was so sad.

My family loved having me around. They were proud of me. They had missed having a mom and wife around to do the regular things I had always done—cook dinner, hang out, play board games, watch movies, take spur-of-the-moment day trips. I enjoyed having the freedom to do those things, too. I'd missed our family life, but I couldn't help feeling that I had a bigger purpose. I'd glimpsed what was possible—to dream big and make a difference. Now, it just felt like I was sitting on the sidelines alone and irrelevant.

When I left the school, I wrote my own announcement in the newsletter that I created each month. I said I was stepping away from the day-to-day operations to pursue my master's degree and ordination in my church. I had dipped my toe into these waters a few times in my life, but something always kept me from continuing. My desire to continue my studies had resurfaced during my time at the school. I wanted to be a bridge between the church and the world. In the months before my departure, I had reentered the master's program, registering for only one online class. Since leaving, I had continued my plan to take one or two online classes each semester, but even that did not seem enough. In my view, the world was rushing by while I was studying.

My drive to achieve—to be a change-maker—was pushing me to get back out there in immediate and concrete ways. Being irrelevant was one of my greatest fears. By the end of the summer, I had given up trying to be still and quiet and had begun a furious pace of networking while taking classes online.

Day after day, I connected with community leaders. I had no problem finding people willing to meet with me. It was reassuring. Everyone I spoke with knew of my work at the school and was interested in helping me find the next step. The problem was that I didn't know what I wanted to do next. I was invited to join several boards and serve as a consultant for a few nonprofit organizations. I tried a few projects, but everything felt dry. I couldn't find anything that inspired me as much as the mission of the school. The Ansley School was my passion. I believed with all my heart that the program could ignite a wave of change in our world. I began to think that I would never find another project that could inspire me as much.

The empty days began to taunt me as they multiplied. I was so anxious. I hated being bored. I hated feeling like I was wasting my life just sitting around at home. I hated that I couldn't figure out how to live in the space and at the pace that I had so deeply desired. I hated that my faith wasn't strong enough to allow me to lean into the present moment. The present just felt like an abyss. I had visions of slowing down, being present, but I just felt restless and irrelevant as the months rolled by. I couldn't find a way to be still.

Each day, when I wasn't in class or studying, I tried to fill my time by tackling one task around the house that I had been putting off. It was January of 2022. On this day, I had decided to go through some of the boxes I had brought from my parents' house. I was sitting in my home office trying to sort through the memories. In the last hour, I had done nothing but move all the photos and memories from one of the boxes into messy piles on my office floor. I still had no idea what to do with all the treasures: my grandfather's college diploma, my grandmother's high school scrapbook (class of 1922), my father's naval uniform, a photo of my mother at a college formal. They were too precious to let go, but all I seemed to be able to do was move them from a box to a pile and, ultimately, back to the box. I was lost in a kaleidoscope of memories when the buzzing of my cell phone broke into the silence. I answered the phone without paying attention to the number on the screen.

"Hello," I said.

"Hi Kate. This is Dr. Jones," answered the voice on the other end of the line.

Dr. Jones was the head of school that The Ansley School board had hired to replace me. She and I had met several times over the summer during her onboarding. She was smart and experienced, and I wanted to do anything I could to be helpful to her during the transition. It had been months since we had spoken.

"The school is hosting a gala in March, and I'd like to do something at the event to honor you," she continued.

An instant rush of gratefulness and foreboding washed over me.

"Did the board ask you to reach out to me?" I asked.

"No," she said. "I just think it would be stupid to host our inaugural gala and not have you a part of it."

I thanked her for her generosity and asked if I could think about it. I really liked her. I hadn't been included in her search or hiring, but I had done all that I could in her early days to get her up to speed. She was kind and experienced and sensitive to my situation. I didn't want her to get mired down in the drama, so we didn't talk much about the details of my departure. I wanted her to develop a healthy and professional relationship with the board, but I was the one with the information she needed to maintain and grow the school day-to-day, so we needed to spend time together. Throughout her first few months, we discussed software systems, passwords, donors, vendors, partners, schedules, staff responsibilities. The list was long because the job was tremendous.

It was generous of her to want to honor me at the gala, but if the board wasn't on board (pardon the pun), then it would be nothing but painful. I feared it would taint her relationship with the board. I also couldn't imagine sitting in a room with everyone and pretending like it was all happy and fine. In the end, I thanked Dr. Jones for thinking of me and explained that I didn't think it was appropriate for me to attend the gala until some healing happened between the board and me. Not surprisingly, we never spoke again.

CHAPTER TWENTY-TWO

"She Tried"

Shame corrodes every part of us that believes
we are capable of change.

–BRENE BROWN

It was almost 7:30 a.m. on a Sunday morning when I pulled into the parking lot of St. Luke's. I'd been invited to preach the sermon at all three services that day as part of my seminary education. I love to preach. The practice of sermon writing is centering for me, and public speaking always gives me joy. There are silly, mundane things that make me nervous like small talk and small rodents, but public speaking is life-giving to me. On this day, though, I was feeling off. The Ansley School gala had been the night before. It was killing me that I had put my all into building the program and that the community came together to celebrate its success without me. My grief was so raw.

"Focus on the gift of today's opportunity," I told myself, as I walked from the parking lot into the building.

It was early, and the building was still quiet. I took a few deep breaths and tried to focus on the joy of the day. The first service was beautiful. As I began to preach, I could feel my tension release. This was where I was supposed to be in this moment. I welcomed the calm, but it didn't last long.

I was coming out of the restroom after the first service and literally ran into a lady who was coming in.

"Oh, hi Kate. The gala last night was so amazing. That school is so incredible. I was surprised you weren't there," she said. "I asked someone, and they said you were out of town. I just couldn't believe you wouldn't be there."

We were standing directly in the doorway of the bathroom. I couldn't breathe. I thought I might pass out.

"I'm glad it was a good evening," I forced myself to say. "I really can't talk about it right now. I need to get ready for the service."

I tried to push my way into the open hall, but she was persistent.

"I just don't understand why you wouldn't go to the event," she continued. "It was amazing, and you're obviously not out of town."

I was feeling desperate and helpless. I looked up and down the hall to find anyone who could save me.

"I'm sorry," I finally said. "I just can't talk about this right now."

I pushed my way through the door and scrambled down the hall, looking for a private place to collect myself. They told people I was out of town. I willed myself to breathe. I needed to get myself together. I was preaching today. It was a big deal for me. I told myself to focus. I closed my eyes and did what I had been doing for years. I pushed the pain way down deep inside and just kept going.

So many people at my church had attended the gala. All of them wanted to talk to me about how amazing it was, and all of them wanted to know why I wasn't there. No one except the board knew the real story. People thought I had stepped away to continue my education, but they assumed that I was also still involved in the school. I was sad and mad, but I didn't want to say anything to disparage the school. It was an amazing program. I wasn't in agreement with how the board was handling the growth and vision, but I believed in the scholars and their families.

To this day, a piece of me breaks inside when someone asks me about the school. I just don't know what to say. My husband encourages me to say that I'm a builder (which is true) and that once the school was up and running, it was time for someone else to come in and run it. It sounds good, but no one seems to be satisfied with that answer.

"But you are on the board, right?" they always say.

"Well, no. I'm giving the program some space," I respond.

People were shocked. They wanted to understand. It didn't seem right. All I wanted to do was crawl into a hole.

One of my neighbors invited a group of friends to go to a concert together for her birthday. Among the guests was one of the original board members. She knew exactly what happened and quietly pulled away from the program about a year after I left. I will never forget the day just a month or so after my departure when she showed up at my doorstep with flowers and a hug. There were really no words for either of us to speak, but I was grateful for her show of friendship and support.

On this summer evening she and I found ourselves in the same Uber heading to the concert. The mood was light and carefree, and then it happened.

"Kate, how's your school going?" asked one of the guests who I only knew in passing.

"I think it's going well," I answered. "I transitioned out a while back."

"Why?" she asked. "You started that school. You worked so hard. How could you leave it?"

I was just trying to breathe. There was no place I could go where the subject of the school didn't come up, and I hadn't found a way to shut it down quickly and gracefully.

"Well, I'm a builder, and it was time for someone to come in who was more interested in running the day-to-day," I said.

"But . . ." she started.

Just then, we arrived at our destination. The doors of the car opened, and the conversation was lost in the flurry of activity as we headed into the concert venue. I knew where it was going, though. I knew all the questions that would've come next. "You're still on the board, right?" "How could you just leave a school you created?" "How could you leave all those children behind?" I was glad not to have to finish the conversation, but the damage had been done. I had to still my mind. I had to gather myself. I had to take deep breaths to keep from falling apart.

Fortunately, my friend who had been on the board appeared by my side.

"I can't believe she asked you those questions," she said. "That was so hard."

"I have that conversation with someone at least once every day. It tears me up every time. I still don't know what to say," I said.

"Wow. I had no idea," she said. "I'm so sorry you have to go through this."

The comment made me feel both supported and alone. Even those who had left with me had turned the page in their lives. They had moved on. I was stuck. I felt like I had no voice. I was scared of the scenarios that people were assuming. Every day, I searched for peace. I wanted people just to stop asking, but I knew that wouldn't happen. The school was a big deal. Even people who didn't know me knew about the school. My identity had become intertwined with the school and finding the point of separation was difficult for everyone—especially me.

The church had always been my safe haven, but now it often felt like a field of land mines. Even though the board hadn't continued a deep relationship with St. Luke's after I left, St. Luke's still claimed and cheered for the school. There was enough overlap that reminders filled the space—the new school vans parked in the church parking lot, an exhibit of the scholars' art hanging in the hallway, announcements for volunteer opportunities. There were days when I wondered if I needed to find a new church home just to find some separation and peace, but I loved my church.

I was greeting people after the service one warm summer Sunday in 2022. I had been gone from the school for almost one year. As the crowd was dwindling, a wonderful woman who had always been one of my biggest supporters came to introduce me to a friend she thought I would like to meet. She made the introduction and was immediately pulled into another conversation. The woman and I had been chatting for a couple of minutes when she mentioned her role as executive director of one of the larger nonprofits that partnered with the school. I'm not sure why I said a word, but before I could stop myself, I said, "Oh, I know several people who work there. You all do a great job."

"How do you know about us?" she asked.

And as if my mouth had a mind of its own, I answered, "I used to work at The Ansley School."

"Oh," she responded. "It's a good thing you left. I heard that the founding director they had over there was a disaster. She was terrible. She didn't know what she was doing. . . ."

Her words continued, but all I heard was the "wamp-wah-wamp-wamp" of the teacher on the Peanuts cartoons. She clearly didn't know who I was. I had to get out of there. I scanned the room around us, but, as usual, I could find no one to save me. My church, my sanctuary, the space where I had always found peace and grounding, was slowly becoming a place I feared.

The next week when I saw the woman at church, our eyes met, and she looked away. I'm not sure if she'd realized who I was and was embarrassed or if she'd realized who I was and didn't want to be seen with me. Either way, it was just one more person, one more place, that brought me to my knees. I was beginning to feel danger everywhere. Would this ever end?

"Is it helpful for you to remind yourself that your grief is normal, and that grief has to run its course?" asked my therapist.

I knew that, but I was still struggling with how to live with the grief and the triggers all around me. What I wanted was to call my mom and dad. I missed them so much.

"Can you name any times when you have felt joy during this time?" she asked.

"I just feel like I had a chance to really make a difference in the world. I feel like God was calling me to do this big thing, and I failed. I feel so guilty. I have let everyone, even God, down," I said. "I told my husband the other night that I guess they could just put on my tombstone: 'She Tried.'"

"But you didn't fail," she reminded me. "You proved to yourself and to the world that you can start a movement for change. The school's still serving all those families. What you did has already changed lives."

I could feel the tears welling in my eyes.

"But I miss it so much," I whispered. "I love it, and I miss it, and I'm so ashamed."

The pain was raw. I couldn't find a way through. I just wanted to breathe and put down the heavy weight of despair. I wanted to be more than the woman who tried. I wanted there to be another chapter to my story. I manically searched for a new path to lead me out of this stuck, sad, and shameful place.

CHAPTER TWENTY-THREE

New Realizations

*I thought being faithful was about becoming
someone other than who I was . . . it wasn't until
I failed that I began to wonder if my human
wholeness might be more useful to God than my
exhausting goodness.*

—BARBARA BROWN TAYLOR

Looking back, I can see the flaw in my thinking, but at the time I was desperate to find another project to take on. I was certain that it would ease my pain. I told myself that when the right thing came up, I would just know. I could jump on board and ease the weight of grief and failure that was slowly crushing me. Day after day,

I kept searching and networking. Small projects popped up here and there, but none of them fed my soul. I needed to find something that would fill the gaping hole in my heart.

It was a Friday in October. I was at the beach for a family wedding when my phone rang. My personal cell number was still the default rollover number for the school. Almost daily, I received calls from vendors and parents looking for the school staff, so when my phone screen showed a call from a number not in my contacts, I let it roll to voicemail and then reluctantly played the recording. This time, though, it wasn't the usual vendor looking for payment or a parent looking for information. This time, it was much different.

"Hi Kate," said the recorded voice. "My name is Susan Jackson. I'm an executive search consultant and have been contracted by an area homeless-serving agency to find an interim executive director to lead their program. Several people have offered your name. Would you be interested in a conversation?"

Before I could stop myself, I was dialing her number. My curiosity overwhelmed any attempt at playing cool. The executive director of a program for children experiencing homelessness was retiring. They were looking for a six-month interim while they searched for a permanent replacement.

"How'd you get my name?" I asked.

"I reached out to several of my networks and your name came up in almost every conversation," she responded.

I would like to say that my ego isn't a driving force in my emotions. I would like to say that I don't care what people think. I would like to say that I know I am a capable and talented woman no matter what others think, but wow. The idea that professionals in the community thought highly of me and my abilities gave me great pleasure. I'm not proud of that, but it was and still is truth for me.

She explained the details of the position, and we planned to meet the next week. For the rest of the weekend, every time the conversation crossed my mind, all I could do was smile and say, "Wow." This position would be proof to me and to the community (especially those who doubted me) that I was doing just fine. I wasn't proud of my desire to "win" and to "be back in the spotlight," but I can't deny its power and influence.

In the end, I didn't accept the position. The decision was difficult, born out of the internal work that I'd been doing since I left The Ansley School. What I loved about my role at the school was the visioning and strategizing. I loved building programs and community partnerships. What drained me during my time at the school was managing staff, reconciling petty cash, and overseeing all the other daily operational pieces of the program. The role of an interim is not to create or build. The role of an interim is to keep the operations going. When I closed my eyes and considered being tied down every day for the next six months running daily operations, I felt no joy. I could definitely do the job and do it really well. Not too long ago, I would have felt compelled to say yes because I believed in their mission, and they needed help. I would have told myself it would be selfish to say no just because I didn't want to do it, but I would be miserable in the day-to-day muck and mud of running an organization. In the end, my quality-of-life concerns won out over my misplaced responsibility. For me, this was something to celebrate.

Not too long after I turned down the interim opportunity, I was offered a position as a consultant for a new community initiative. My role would be to raise money and awareness for a community housing crisis impacting working families. The hours were flexible. It didn't require me to be in an office, and there was a support staff to do the administrative pieces of the project. All I had to do was advocate for the program in the community. My excitement was unbridled. This was a perfect role for me. It was a mission I believed to be so important, and a role that suited me perfectly. I jumped right in.

In the months since my departure from the school, I had grown significantly. I was much more sure of what I wanted (or at least much more sure of what I didn't want). I was much more confident in my expertise and my gifts. It was empowering. I learned to set and protect my boundaries. More importantly, I could do it without feeling guilty or undeserving.

The work with the nonprofit offered me the opportunity to have a flexible schedule—to continue my slow progression of online classes and have time for my family. And it gave me the chance to participate on panels and speak publicly to large groups. I love speaking in public. I love to share stories. I jumped at every invitation to speak. It was life-giving to me. The problem was that almost every speech turned to my work at The Ansley School. It was the thing in my bio that piqued everyone's interest.

"Can you tell us about the school you started?" the graduate student in the classroom asked.

"Sure," I said, as I explained the tragedy of young children falling through the cracks in the system and my determination to find a solution. I was presenting at an event hosted by a nearby university.

No one in the audience could tell that I was dying on the inside. I was really good at keeping the smile on my face and the confidence in my voice, but every time, a tiny piece of me crumbled. The school would always be my ultimate passion. For me, it was the cause above all causes, and people loved it. They wanted to know more. And without fail, the inevitable question always came.

"Why did you step away from the program?"

I have yet to come up with a response that satisfies the community or me. It's just crushing and complicated.

It was early evening in July of 2023, and I was sitting in a pub with two potential funders for the new project I was supporting. Ironically, one had been on the board of the school during my tenure, and the other was a new member of the board.

As we sipped our beers, I shared the mission and need of my newest venture. The staff had created a compelling and professional packet, which I shared with my friends. They were inspired by the work, and the conversation flowed from the business at hand to catching up on life.

"So, let me tell you all about what is happening at the school," said the current board member.

"You know," I interrupted, "my departure from the school wasn't pretty, and it's really hard for me to talk about it."

He was visibly stunned.

"I had no idea," he said. "I think maybe you have the wrong impression. What if I tell them you want to come back?"

"No," said the other friend at the table. "I was there. There was a movement to push her out. The damage is irrevocable."

His response both crushed me and filled me with relief. The admission had shifted the air in the room. For me, it was a gift for someone to speak the words on my behalf. For our friend, it was a shocking complication.

"OK, well," the current board member said, "I'm not sure what to think of this. The organization is doing amazing work."

"I hope the best for the program. I love the families and the scholars," I said. "It breaks my heart that I can't be part of it, but I don't want to be a distraction."

There was a moment of uncomfortable silence before we paid our bill and headed out of the restaurant. I had a feeling that the conversation had permanently altered my friendship with both men. It had been more than two years since I left, and still the school remained a wound in my soul that was constantly ripped open. It didn't matter what role I had or what project I was championing. The hole in my soul left by the absence of The Ansley School could not be filled simply by finding a way to build my ego or feel relevant. I realized in that moment that the wound wasn't created by a loss of status or projects. The wound was created by a deep grief—a loss of something I truly loved, something I truly believed in. The wound was caused by the ominous feeling that I had failed God.

CHAPTER TWENTY-FOUR
All for the Children

If we are to teach real peace in this world,
and if we are to carry on a real war against war,
we shall have to begin with the children.

—MAHATMA GANDHI

I sat on the porch of the two-story house in west Atlanta. It was familiar to me, but I still felt like an outsider. Most of the young adults coming and going didn't acknowledge me, but that was OK. I wasn't here to visit them. I was here to see the youngest of the family, Trameka and Tramarkes. It was their ninth birthday. I had known the twins and their parents since they enrolled in the first pre-K class of The Ansley School in 2018. They were now about to start the fourth grade.

Their lives had been a series of struggles. Over the years, the parents had shared pieces of their story with me. The Stinsons had been married for years and had nine children. Mr. Stinson was disabled and had been unable to work since an accident at work in 2016. Almost immediately, the family of eleven found themselves on the verge of being evicted from their two-bedroom home. The house was infested with rats and black mold, but it was the only place they had to call home. The day before their eviction, an Atlanta-based celebrity heard their story and gave them a five-bedroom furnished house to live in for free for the next year.

The day of the move, there were cameras and reporters. The celebrity was there to welcome them to their new home. Mr. Stinson kept the video loaded on his phone and was ready to show it to anyone who would watch. The twins were only seventeen months old at the time. On the video, they enter the house perched shyly on their parent's hips. They are so cute and so little. The older children race through the house claiming rooms and testing out the beds. It seems like a new beginning. The video ends with the family waving and smiling from their new miracle home—but living on the edge of homelessness is complicated. Two years later, the twins would only remember the home that saved them from the street from the video taken on that first day. When the year was up, the family had no way to pay for the house. They found themselves back on the streets, literally sleeping on the sidewalk, until they could find a shelter to take a family of eleven.

The only shelter they found to take the whole family was almost worse than the streets. Running water and electricity were unpredictable. There was rampant disease, gang violence, and sex trafficking. The living conditions were disgusting. The old brick building stood across the street from St. Luke's and Crossroads—the homeless-serving agency where, at the time, I was serving as board chair. In 2017, only a few months after the family moved into the shelter, it was permanently closed by the city. Crossroads was asked to organize a transition for all the residents.

As board chair, I got an insider's view of the facility. I'd heard rumors about the living conditions but not until I went inside to help with some transitions did I fully understand. Buckets of human waste were tucked in almost every corner. Extension cords snaked up through floorboards from overloaded adapters. Old mattresses littered the floor. When I entered the building, I slapped my hand over my nose and mouth as the heat and the smell assaulted me. I had to fight the threat of tears and my roiling stomach as I walked around and thought about all the people who had no choice but to call this home. I couldn't imagine anyone living there. I hadn't even met the Stinson family yet.

Homelessness is complicated. The residents of the shuttered shelter who were willing were placed in other housing and connected with case managers. Sadly, for some, trust issues, fear, and disillusionment kept them from accepting any help. Because the Stinson family was so large, the city placed them in a subsidized house on the west side of Atlanta. They were also assigned a case worker to support them. It was their case worker who reached out to The Ansley School in the late summer of 2018 to inquire about our new program and the possibility of enrolling the family's youngest twins. Little did I know that I would build a relationship with that family that would stand the test of time.

It was Mr. Stinson who had apologized to me on the first day of school for coming in with alcohol on his breath. At the time, I only knew a small part of their story, but the twins had already found a special place in my heart. They were so small, and they struggled in the classroom. Like so many of the scholars in our program, they had very low language exposure, but high exposure to street violence. Living on the streets is traumatic for everyone, but for children without the ability to express their emotions, the trauma only multiplies.

Tramarkes was boy through and through. He was energetic and rambunctious. He cussed and hit and kicked and talked about things that no four-year-old should know. He was the class clown. Everything he did was big and loud and cool to his fellow classmates. He was street smart and hung out with all his older brothers and their friends. The other kids in the class looked up to him. They wanted to be his friend. They thought he was cool.

Trameka was quiet and shy. She turned into herself as she tried to make sense of the world. While her brother was making friends and being the cool kid in class, Trameka spent most of the day hiding under the table. The other children taunted her for not talking. Every attempt to lure her out from under the table ended in a match of kicking and screaming.

"We need some help down here," yelled their teacher, Ms. Rami, from the classroom door one day during our first year.

Her tone was urgent. I got up from my desk and raced down the hall. It was chaos. The assistant teacher was in the corner. Her ear was bleeding. Ms. Rami was trying to calm the rowdy classroom.

"I tried to coax Trameka out from under the table, and she kicked me and ripped out my earring," explained the assistant teacher as she tried to collect herself.

As Ms. Rami worked to calm the other students in her kind and quiet way, I went to talk with Trameka.

"Hi," I said as I sat myself on the floor next to the table. "I know you don't want to come out, but hurting your teacher isn't nice."

She was quiet. Her eyes were staring straight through me.

"Trameka," I continued. "Want to come down the hall with me? We can color or have a snack."

I offered her my hand. She moved just a little, and I thought she was going to take it. Then the pain hit me like a shot. Trameka kicked me hard in the shin. As I reared back, she scrambled out from under the table and bolted out the door. I knew not to run after her. That only creates more running. I took a deep breath and ignored the throbbing in my leg as I calmly followed Trameka out into the hall just as she reached the door to exit our floor. The doors were too tall and heavy for the children to open without an adult. Unfortunately, a church staff person happened to be entering the door from the other direction just as Trameka arrived. The small girl bolted through the open door and up the stairs. My panic was building. I began to run behind her taking the stairs two at a time.

"Trameka," I called. "This is not safe. You need to stop."

I exited the stairs to the hallway just as Trameka ducked behind the water fountain. The door to the outside was just around the corner. I took a deep breath and walked slowly toward her hiding place. I positioned myself between the water fountain and the door before I began to speak.

"Trameka, you're not being safe. Will you come . . ."

I didn't even finish my sentence when she burst out of her hiding place and ran right into me in an attempt to escape. I put my arms around her as gently as I could. She struggled and then looked me directly in the eyes.

"Fucking cunt," she said.

Her big brown eyes and tiny, innocent features were completely incongruent with the words that had just come out of her mouth. She struggled in my arms. Restraining a child was never recommended, but I knew if I let her go, she would run out of the building. I held her in my arms and slid down the wall until I was seated on the floor. I was at a loss. I was stunned and frustrated. My heart was racing. I felt like I was in over my head. I had no idea what the next move should be. This precious angel and her brother were filled with so much rage and trauma and anguish. Once again, I was reminded of why we began this journey. We knew it wouldn't be easy, but I had no idea the depth of commitment and trust from both children and adults, staff, and parents it would take to make this work. Then, all of a sudden, as the thoughts raced through my head matching only the rapid beat of my heart, I felt Trameka begin to relax in my arms. We both let out a long breath that we'd been holding. I cradled her in my arms and quickly carried her downstairs.

In the classroom, things had calmed considerably. The assistant teacher had bandaged her ear. The earring had not split her lobe, thank goodness. The class was back to their regular activities. I called Trameka's mother and explained the situation. She was apologetic and frustrated. She was afraid her children would be asked to leave.

"No," I said. "We'll find a way to handle this as a team. You're part of that team."

And to think, I assumed that once the school was up and running, the teachers would be good to handle the days without other staff around. This crisis had taken all of us to handle, and even though it was a big one, it was only one of many.

In the end, we worked with the family and our partners in trauma care to set up individual plans for both children. Trameka was so smart. With the extra attention and special work with trauma counselors, she began to come out of her shell. She loved to draw and look at books. She still spent a lot of time alone, but she was no longer hiding under the table. Tramarkes, on the other hand, was still king of the classroom. All the other scholars loved him. He was working on boundaries and appropriate words for school. His biggest struggle was academic. He had no interest in coloring or looking at books. He didn't like reading time or table time. His fine motor skills were almost nonexistent. As frustrated as his sister was that she couldn't make friends, Tramarkes was equally frustrated that he couldn't complete classroom assignments.

Their home life was rough. Mr. Stinson suffered from a number of debilitating conditions including epilepsy, bipolar disorder, schizophrenia, and neuropathy. He was often unable to afford his medication and tried to handle his pain with his own variety of numbing. He spent some time in jail. Mrs. Stinson had her own health problems plus a husband and nine children to care for. She loved her family fiercely, but she could only do so much. The older children were getting into trouble on a regular basis, and the older they got, the more serious the fallout became. But Trameka and Tramarkes were at school every day. In their first year, neither twin missed even one day of school. Every day, rain, snow, or sleet, their parents walked them a mile to the subway station, rode the train with them to the nearest stop, and took a bus to the school. Perfect attendance.

The twins thrived in the school. Their parents were active in our school community. One day, Mr. Stinson showed up in a suit at drop-off.

"Wow," said one of our staff members. "What's the occasion?"

"My parole officer said I have to go to anger management classes," he said. "So, I thought I'd wear a suit to make a good impression."

The whole staff smiled at his renewed commitment.

When I left the school in 2021, Trameka had become one of the top readers in the class. She had a small group of friends and was well-liked by all her peers. She was a girly-girl. She loved everything pink and glittery. Tramarkes had calmed considerably. He understood boundaries much better and had learned new ways to handle his anger, but he was still struggling mightily with academics.

The Stinson family and I stay in touch. I visit as often as I can, and here I was on the twins' ninth birthday sitting on their porch in absolute awe of how big they were getting. Mr. Stinson came out to greet me but then retreated back into the house. He loved his children and his wife, but life was hard for him. Mrs. Stinson sat with me on the porch as her older children moved in and out of the house. They were mostly young adults now, but none of them had the resources to launch, so they remained at home.

The birthday twins eagerly opened the gifts I had brought. Glittery makeup, lots of pink jewelry and some girl-power outfits for Trameka. A Lego set, some shorts and T-shirts, and a mini punching bag (by request) for Tramarkes. Even after all these years together, I still felt a little unsure sitting on their porch. I still wonder what they see when they look at me. The rich white lady who gives them stuff? I'd like to think they see me as an ally and a friend because that's how I see them. Our paths have been so different, and the disparity of our opportunities is vast and unfair. I have a friend who likes to say that she and I were born into the "lucky sperm club," and I think that about sums it up. There's no more rhyme or reason to it than that.

Generational poverty is like quicksand. The idea that any one person can just "pull themselves up by their bootstraps" is flawed. Sure, sometimes it works, but the hole is deep and sticky. Breath by breath and inch by inch, you work to keep yourself afloat just enough to get by. I don't want my relationship with the Stinsons to be based on a power dynamic. I care about them—especially those twins—and I want to see them break free from the circumstances and the systems that have haunted their family for so many generations. I passionately believe that educational opportunity is the way to create lasting change.

As I chatted with Mrs. Stinson, we watched Trameka glitter up her face with her new makeup, sneaking shy peeks at herself in the iPad selfie camera on the table. She was truly a princess. As our conversation continued, I turned my attention toward Tramarkes. He was being awfully quiet, and history had taught me that that might be a problem. This time, though, I was absolutely wrong.

Tramarkes sat on the floor surrounded by parts and pieces of his new punching bag. The complicated directions were opened beside him, and he was sorting the pieces into groups.

"Can I help you with that, Tramarkes?" I asked.

He was immersed in the project and didn't even look up.

"You know, he got best reader in his class this year," said his mother, smiling.

"What?" I exclaimed. "That's amazing. Tramarkes, I'm so impressed with you."

"Uh-huh," he replied without looking up.

By the time I left that day, Tramarkes had read the directions and assembled the entire punching bag and stand, all by himself.

"Wow," I exclaimed. "I'm so proud of both of you. I can't believe how fast you're growing up."

They both beamed at me. Trameka gave me a huge hug, wrapping her feet around my waist. Tramarkes was too cool but gave me a sly little smile. This is why I dreamed the school into existence. I wanted to create a place for children like these precious angels to be offered the chance to escape the quicksand of generational poverty. Here was living proof that what I built was making a difference. Trameka and Tramarkes talk of going to high school and college one day. They have a whole community supporting them and their family as they grow. The speech I had made to the scholars on the last day of pre-K remained true.

"Take a look around you," I had said to our young scholars. "Look beside you. Look behind you. Look in front of you. No matter where you go in your life, these people will always have your back. Never forget that you're part of a community that loves and supports you today and always. You'll never have to be alone."

CHAPTER TWENTY-FIVE
Keep Dreaming

*The best and most beautiful things in the
world cannot be seen or even touched—
they must be felt with the heart.*

—HELEN KELLER

The world had moved on while I was busy building the school. I had tried to jump back in, but I was failing miserably. In retrospect, even though I felt bored and irrelevant, I was doing a lot—seminary classes, fundraising, consulting. Still, I couldn't find a way past the grief. Even two years later, there was nowhere I could go that someone didn't ask me about the school. It still made me physically ill, which made me angry with myself.

"Just get over it," I told myself every day. "What's wrong with you?"

Then I had an epiphany.

"I had an epiphany in therapy," I said to my sister one day on the phone.

"Oh, tell me. I can't wait to hear," she said expectantly.

She and I loved the process of therapy. We loved learning about the inner workings of our minds. There isn't a personality test that we haven't taken and analyzed. During this time of intense grief, therapy had become a lifeline for me. I looked forward to it more than anything. It was one of the few things that gave me a boost.

"I realized today that my coping mechanism is over-functioning," I exclaimed.

There was a beat of silence before she replied, "No shit, Sherlock. Was that it? Are you just realizing that?"

My husband, as well, had a similar reaction.

I like to think of myself as very self-aware, but somehow this one had eluded me. I never thought of myself as *over-*functioning. Getting stuff done is just what I do. It's my superpower. I find it energizing and productive. People are often wowed by my capacity to do stuff. When I feel down or frustrated, conquering a giant to-do list always puts me right. I took on the skill as my responsibility and call in the world. Apparently, all that time, it wasn't only my superpower but my kryptonite.

The compounded grief of the past few years that had embedded in my soul was, for the first time, too big and deep to be fixed by even the most accomplished over-functioning.

"Just be" was the mantra that played again and again in my head. "Walk the earth." "Slow down." That's what all the books say. I could build a school. I could raise a million dollars. I could run a household and a school board. I could give birth to four children, but I couldn't sit still. What was wrong with me?

"What would you tell a friend who was sharing this story with you?" my therapist asked as I sat in her office one day.

Her office was in a quaint guest house behind a large main house. It was filled with light and comfort and books. Just walking into the space helped me breathe.

"Well," I said. "I always tell people who are struggling to be gentle with themselves."

"Maybe you could tell yourself the same," she suggested.

"It's so boring. I just sit around. It feels like I'm just wallowing in pain," I argued.

"So, how is what you're doing working out for you?" she asked with a knowing smile.

"It's not the same thing," I argued.

"OK," she said doubtfully. "Does being gentle with yourself have to mean sitting around?" she asked.

In my mind, gentle always meant slow and still. Gentle meant nestled on a comfortable sofa with a cup of tea and a good book or sitting by a river looking at the view. I'd tried all of this, and I'd heard it all. "Keep trying." "Give it time." I'd given it time. It didn't work for me, but neither did my manic need to do things—to make a difference. So, maybe gentle looks different for everyone. Maybe gentle means listening to the unique call of the soul.

I don't think I was made to be still for very long, but I also don't think I was made to do everything in my path that needs to be done. In the wise words of self-proclaimed "recovering lawyer" and writer, Bob Goff: "We don't need to do what we're merely capable of doing. The trick is to figure out what we were made to do."[15]

When I *over*-function, I am actually exploiting my gifts. We're all at our best when we're operating at the speed of our souls—a concept I borrow from writer Shauna Niequist.[16] These words released me from my self-imposed pressure to be still. I needed to find the unique pace of my own soul. For me, it started with acknowledging how I was feeling and letting that be OK. Some days, I feel like being still, so I relax into a good book or a good Netflix binge. Some days I feel like being still, but I have responsibilities and commitments, so I do my stuff, and acknowledge that that day will not be one of my favorites. Many days, I feel like getting stuff done, so I do my stuff but pay attention to the amount of joy each task brings.

In the fall of 2022, I was having one of those days when I was feeling strong and hopeful. Without even realizing it, I'd had a string of days where I wasn't completely weighed down by grief. I was finally beginning to find some peace. It wasn't because of anything specific that I was doing. It was just a shift I noticed. The moments of peace and lightness were fragile and fleeting, but, slowly, they were becoming more regular in my life. I was beginning to find the rhythm of my soul. So, when the email popped into my inbox, I didn't immediately go into panic mode. The subject read: "Connecting with Kate Kennedy." It was forwarded to me by the priest at a church that had welcomed me as a guest preacher. There was no context provided. The priest had simply added me to the string and forwarded the message. Curious, I began to scroll down the page. The message read:

> It was a pleasure to worship with you all last Sunday. I always enjoy attending your church when visiting my daughter and her family in Atlanta. I also appreciate you taking the time to talk with me about my desire to connect with The Ansley School founder Kate Kennedy as I help a church in my own Pittsburgh Diocese.

My stomach tightened.

"Not again," I thought with a loud sigh.

I paused, wondering if I wanted to just delete it. Or, maybe this was different, I decided. So, slowly I returned my eyes to the computer screen and continued reading. The woman had written:

> I am still a bit stunned at the small world-ness of this connection and I am truly delighted in God's reach into these types of details. Coincidence? Perhaps. But I believe it is more than that and I am grateful. Below is the email I had sent to Kate a little less than two weeks ago and then received an automated response that she had taken a leave. Thanks for helping us to connect and whatever works easiest is good.

I had to read the text a few times to understand what was happening. Slowly, realization dawned on me, and my heart lightened just a touch.

The message was from a woman from Pennsylvania who happened to be visiting the church the day that I preached. Recently, she had organized a small group of women to build a preschool for children experiencing homelessness in Pittsburgh. She had researched similar programs online and found The Ansley School website and my email. When the email was returned, she thought she had hit a dead end, until she visited her daughter on that Sunday morning in her Atlanta church. There I was—the guest preacher for the day.

I couldn't deny the divine providence in the message and the event, but it was still so difficult to talk about the school. I debated how to respond. In the end, it was just too providential to ignore, and I was feeling stronger. So, we set up a time to talk by phone.

I wasn't looking forward to trying to explain my departure from the school again. We had to reschedule a couple of times because of life getting in the way. By the time we finally connected one sunny afternoon, I was feeling pretty nonchalant about the whole thing. Just one more conversation like so many I had had before. I could get it done and move on.

"In full disclosure, I want to let you know right up front, that I'm no longer connected with the school," I said, feeling a little surprised at the calm and confidence in my voice. "I don't really want to go into the details, but I just wanted you to know that before we got too far into the conversation."

"I appreciate that," she responded. "I'm sure it wasn't an easy decision. If it's OK, I'd still love your advice and guidance as the original founder."

Wow. That was the most healthy and supportive exchange about my relationship with the school that I had experienced. I was still apprehensive about the conversation, but my shoulders relaxed a little. She went on to explain her vision and ask my advice on the process and next steps. As we spoke, I realized that I had let the ugly ending of my relationship with the school overshadow the beautiful work that I had led. In telling her the story, I realized, maybe for the first time, the miracle of what we had done.

Who just goes out and starts a school? When I was in the process, I was too close to see the enormity of our success. Sharing the story from the beginning helped me more fully appreciate the wonder of our achievements. From the beginning, I had dreamed of creating a blueprint for others to start similar programs in their neighborhoods. I had a blueprint, and now I had been given the gift of offering it to someone as passionate as I was.

Over the next weeks and months, I met regularly via Zoom and telephone with the Pittsburgh committee of women. They reminded me so much of our founding group—very strong, opinionated, stubborn women who wanted to honor the potential and dignity of every child. They were truly amazing. There's a special sort of passion that exists within women that, when harnessed, can make the impossible possible. The only thing that stands between passionate women and real change is the courage to take the first step.

I'd taken that first step, and now these women wanted to take one, too. I hoped I could offer them wisdom that might ease some of the doubt.

"We're hosting a gathering for parents to come learn about our program," offered one of the women on our Zoom call.

They went on to tell me all about the plans and logistics for the event. They had covered all the bases. They were doing all the right things, just as we'd done during the summer before we opened our doors.

"I just want you to know," I shared with them, "that the first time we set up a recruiting event, no one came."

I watched their faces drop.

"Don't give up, though," I said. "I was devastated after the first and second and third time that no one showed any interest, but we just kept plugging away. Homelessness is complicated. The parents have so much to worry about that's more pressing than preschool. Hang in there. If you build a good program, they will come."

The email I received the day after their event was disappointing but not surprising. It read:

> No one showed up. We're so glad we talked
> to you ahead of time.

So many times, when we were building The Ansley School, we felt uncertain. There were so many naysayers and doubters. Sometimes, it felt like pushing a rock up a hill only to have it roll back down over us. Now, though,

I could offer this group a small cushion of hope. I could offer guidance and advice on what to do and what not to do. Community by community, we can change the face of educational inequity. This is not work for do-gooders. This is work for change-makers. It's hard and messy. It takes strength, stamina, and fortitude. I'm honored to be able to shed light onto the new, unknown paths these women are forging in their community. I hope to be able to watch this concentric circle grow to communities across the globe.

It was mid-October of 2023. We were sitting at one of our favorite local Mexican restaurants. Chips and salsa. Tacos and margaritas. The table was filled with food and drinks. Around me sat most of the staff who had worked for me at The Ansley School. We used to call ourselves the "A team." For many of them, working at the school had been one of their first "real" jobs. It wasn't a typical job. The work was hard. The organization was new. Every time we did something, it was the first time. Now they had all moved on. I was so proud of each of them. They were all smart and successful with great careers. They were bringing their special passion and vision to schools and nonprofits across Atlanta.

We'd kept in touch over the past few years, but this was the first time we'd all gotten together. We laughed and shared memories. We talked about complicated endings and beautiful beginnings. They were proud of what we'd created. They were glad we'd walked the path together. We were all thrilled to have the "A team" back together. We had done something that no one thought could be done, and though none of us was still there, the program we created was standing on its own.

As we sat there laughing and talking, I thought about the globe that now sat on my desk at home—the one that had been given to me by one of the "A team" on the last day of our first year of school with a note he had attached: "I believe you will start schools like this all over the world, and I will help you."

I realized at that moment that I was doing just that. The group in Pittsburgh was still moving forward. The leader and I were making plans to present the model at a national convention. I didn't fail. My dream had come true. My dream was never to run a school. My dream was to jumpstart a movement. The dream was for a community to come together and create a new path of hope and opportunity. Because I dared to chase a dream, Trameka and Tramarkes and all the other scholars and their families now have a community of people who have their backs. Now, it looks like the children of Pittsburgh will have the same opportunity. Who knows how far this vision might spread? I can't wait to keep dreaming.

EPILOGUE

*Miracles in fact are a retelling in small letters of the
very same story which is written across the whole
world in letters too large for some of us to see.*

–C. S. LEWIS

Someone once asked me if I had known when I started The Ansley School all that I know now, would I do it again? The answer is a resounding, "Yes." At first, my "yes" was only in response to the good that the school is doing in the world. The difference the program has made in the lives of so many children in the few short years it has been operating is solid proof that the mission is changing the landscape of opportunity. Even in my hurt, I could clearly see the extraordinary good in that. Over time, though, I began to understand another reason for my "yes."

I would do it all over again, also, because I have learned that wandering in darkness has the power to teach us more about who we are than any other experience. The semidarkness and shadow-filled moments that had dotted my life prior to founding the school were of little help to me. I could *over*-function any shadow time back into the light, but this darkness was so much deeper.

I don't think any of us like the dark places too much. They are painful and scary. We work hard to avoid them or at least get out of them as quickly as possible. My wise friend the Reverend Winnie Varghese reminded me that we are "light turning on people." We have so much access to light that we don't always understand the gift of darkness. "The darkness," she says, "is not a void. It is a depth, a place that we are invited to sit."[17] Only in the darkness can we see the stars.

There was darkness before there was light. Darkness is a given, and in so many ways, a gift. The sprouting of tiny plants, the explosive beginning of a new star, the birth of a newborn baby—all new life begins in darkness and pushes into the light. Without darkness, there is no light. Without darkness, there are no miracles.

There was a parent at The Ansley School who declared each Monday to be "Miracle Monday." While most were dragging and slow on Monday mornings, she would always burst through the doors reminding everyone that miracles happen on Monday.

Her life wasn't easy. If anyone was in need of a life-changing miracle, it was her. She and her two boys bounced from shelter to shelter. Each day she needed to wrestle her way up a mountain simply to meet the basic needs of her family. Her boys' father showed up when he needed something but was otherwise absent. Life was really hard and lonely for her, but on Mondays, she expected miracles . . . and she was never disappointed.

Each Tuesday, I asked her to share her miracles with me. They were usually very small—someone offered her a seat on a crowded bus; she wasn't late picking up her boys from school; the breakfast at the shelter tasted extra delicious. Some days she could find no more than the fact that she woke up, but she celebrated it as a gift. Even in the deep darkness and despair of her life, she was determined to find joy at least one day per week. Her enthusiasm was contagious. Miracle Mondays are now a part of my family life.

When I was building the school, I noticed and celebrated miracle after miracle. Even on the hardest days, the hand of God was hard to miss. But when I left the school, the darkness descended. I could find nothing but pain and loss. As is my way, I tried to turn on the light and keep going, but the bulb had gone out, and I wasn't able to replace it on my own. I spent a lot of time trying and failing to reach and replace that one light bulb all by myself. I felt alone. I was acting like I was alone, but I wasn't. Once I stopped focusing on replacing that light bulb, I began to notice the subtle and not-so-subtle shafts of light around me. They were there to lift me up and show me a new way, but I was too busy focusing on fixing that one light bulb to notice.

The circumstances of my departure from the school were not what I wanted, but my journey has taught me so much about who I am and who I am meant to be. I hope the school will go on to be a miracle in the lives of so many children and their parents. When I look at that, I realize the magnitude of the greater story. It reminds me of sonder—the word I introduced in the prologue—a word that describes the realization that we are all bit players in the stories of those we meet.

Our stories intersect in so many ways. Everything we are influences everyone around us in ways we may never fully understand. I move forward to live the rest of my story with the hope that it will add to the beauty of the world in some small way.

By May of 2023, I had finally gathered enough credits to earn a master's degree in theology. I loved it so much that I'm now a doctoral candidate in a program focused on creative writing and public theology, while continuing to work with groups of people around the country who dream of re-creating the Ansley model in their communities. This is a beautiful path I found only through embracing and living out the tapestry of me. I hope that my path will create a miracle for others along the way because miracles remind us that we're not alone.

We all have the capacity to make lasting community change in our own unique ways if we can find the strength and courage to take the first step and keep on walking. Sometimes the changes are broad and sweeping, and sometimes they are simply small shifts in perspective, but through them all, we create a more vibrant and beautiful world. We can never underestimate the impact we have on one another.

The work is hard, and no one can do it alone. Real change requires us to challenge the status quo, to lean into the deepest hopes and dreams of all those we meet, and to be willing to wander in the darkness. Only in the darkness are we able to envision our community and ourselves through a new light. Only by living out our stories are we able to be part of the greater narrative.

This story is not just the story of me, but it's also the story of us. It's the story of what can happen when we gratefully embrace both the light and the darkness, when we recognize the beauty and complexities of our own lives, and when we learn to appreciate the value of how these experiences give us opportunities to grow, change, and impact each other. It's the story of living into the full experience of dreaming big, falling hard, and bouncing back.

May today there be peace within you.
May you trust God that you are exactly where you are meant to be.
May you not forget the infinite possibilities that are born in faith.
May you use those gifts that you have received and pass on the
love that has been given to you.
May you be content knowing you are a child of God.
Let this presence settle into your bones and allow your soul
the freedom to sing, dance, praise, and love.
It is there for each and every one of us.

—ST. THERESE OF LISIEUX

EXERCISES FOR DEEPER EXPLORATION

Exploring Through a Lens of Social Impact

1. What resources exist for children without stable
    housing in your community?
    [For more information on education and homelessness,
    I invite you to visit the National Center for Homeless
    Education at https://nche.ed.gov/data-and-stats/]

2. What resources exist for children with learning
    differences in your community?

3. Can you identify systems that create or diminish
    equity in your community?

4. In his book, *Toxic Charity*, Robert Lupton argues
    that sometimes efforts to help only serve to make
    the "doers" feel better about themselves. Research
    organizations in your community that you believe are

doing true change-making work? How do you know?
(Chapter 4)

5. What is the relationship between law enforcement
and marginalized populations in your community?
Consider how we can work together to build bridges.
(Chapter 11)

6. The original mission of the school was "to help
families break the cycle of generational poverty by
providing children with an excellent education and
collaborative family support in a nurturing and faith-
inspired environment." We decided to use "faith-
inspired" rather than "faith-based." The curriculum
was secular, but a multi-faith thread ran through the
program. The school lost out on some funding because
of religious issues. For some, the program was not
Christian enough, and for others, the program was
too Christian. A third group wanted no connection
to any faith tradition. What are your thoughts on
this subject? How do religion and culture affect one
another?

Exploring Through a Lens of Personal Growth

1. Have you ever felt a nudging in your heart to do something that seemed impossible? How did you respond?

2. Can you name a time when you had to trust the process and just lean in? How did it feel?

3. Create a timeline of major events and themes in your life. Can you identify any "threads" that have run through your life? How do these "threads" weave together in you to create the person that you are? (Chapter 2)

4. If you are a parent, what are your greatest hopes and fears for your children? Can you identify any "threads" running through your children's lives? How do your tapestries weave together? What might you learn from each other? (Chapter 3)

5. Make a list of the ways you serve or are served in your community. What ways are you creating and/or receiving long-term change? (Chapter 4)

6. What societal narratives keep you from fully believing in yourself? How do they affect your ability to live out your dreams? (Chapter 5)

7. Think of someone you know who is completely different from you (i.e., economically, racially, religiously, educationally, ideologically, etc.). Imagine how they might see you through their eyes. Notice how you see them. (Chapter 10)

8. Do you know your Enneagram type? How does it help you understand yourself?
   [For more information on the Enneagram, I invite you to visit https://www.enneagraminstitute.com (Chapter 13)]

9. What parts of your story do you struggle with the most? What parts of your story help you feel like you belong? (Chapter 16)

10. Create a space for people to come together and share their stories with one another. How does it feel? What might we learn from the process? Reflect on places your stories connect.

Exploring Through a Lens of Theological Reflection

1. How do you understand God's work in the world?

2. What role does relationship play in serving one another?

3. Pope John Paul II believed that no one is so poor they have nothing to give, and no one is so rich they have nothing to receive. What does this mean to you? What are some ways we can live this out in the world?

4. Think of a time you felt the hand of God in your life. How did you know? How did you respond? [For more information on Clearness Committees, I invite you to visit https://couragerenewal.org/library /the-clearness-committee-a-communal-approach-to -discernment/ (Chapter 18)]

5. Reflect on a time you have been called to sit in the darkness. How did you grow?

6. Reflect on how you understand God's presence in the darkness and/or God's power over darkness.

7. Create a space for people to come together and share their stories with one another. How does this feel like a holy space? What insights might we gain from the process? Reflect on places that your stories connect.

ACKNOWLEDGEMENTS

I am so grateful for all the amazing people who have walked this path with me. There is no way to name them all because every person, both those known to me and those who simply started a ripple from afar that formed my path, have led me to this moment. Sonder is a holy, real, and miraculous force. Know that I am in awe of the way God works in the world and thankful to both those I name and all those whose names I may never know.

To my family:

Robert—the only person who has been able to hold my attention for thirty-plus years, the love of my life, and the foundation of our family—and John Robert, Crawford, Sam, and Katherine Claire, my beautiful and wise children, who support my dreams and my moods and offer me more love and inspiration than they will ever know.

To my sisters, Elizabeth and Mary Crawford, without whom I would be lost.

To Jesica Eames whose wisdom and presence have formed me in more ways than I can express.

To Kathy Izard, Elizabeth Dickens, Debra Nichols, and Sarah Lahay—the amazing team who inspired, coached, edited, proofread, designed, and supported this project in so many ways.

To my beta readers, Molly Marrah, the Reverend Winnie Varghese, Jill Joplin, and my husband Robert who made it through the first draft of this manuscript and came back for more.

To the staff and community of St. Luke's Episcopal Church in Atlanta and Crossroads for their support and belief in my dreams.

To all the donors, supporters, believers, and fellow dreamers who supported the vision in tangible ways.

To the Reverend Winnie Varghese, who (for reasons I will never know) believed in me from the day we met and has supported me in more ways than she will ever know.

And, finally, to all the beautiful children and families of The Ansley School who trusted us enough to join this amazing journey. You are the reason.

ENDNOTES

1   Koenig, John. 2021. *The Dictionary of Obscure Sorrows*. New York: Simon and Schuster.

2   I had originally used pseudonyms for the Stinson family, but because their story is so unique and so many details are included, I wanted to obtain their blessing on what I was sharing. I visited them one afternoon on their front porch and read them what I had written. They asked me to use their real names because they believe that their story and their lives will offer hope to others. It was important to them to claim their story, maybe for the first time.

3   "Educating Children and Youth Experiencing Home-lessness." n.d. https://nche.ed.gov/wp-content/uploads/2023/05/AnnotatedResearchSummaryReport-2023.pdf

4   John 10:10 (NRSV).

5   Lupton, Robert D. 2011. *Toxic Charity: How Churches and Charities Hurt Those They Help (and How to Reverse It)*. New York: HarperOne.

6   Sparks, Sarah D. 2016. "Student Mobility: How It Affects Learning." *Education Week*. August 11, 2016. https://www.edweek.org/leadership/student-mobility-how-it–affects-learning/2016/08

7   "The Enneagram Institute." n.d. The Enneagram Institute. https://www.enneagraminstitute.com

8   "What Does the Research Say about the Relationship between Reading Proficiency by the End of Third Grade and Academic Achievement, College Retention, College and Career Readiness, Incarceration, and High School Dropout?" n.d. Ies.ed.gov. https://ies.ed.gov/ncee/rel/Products/Region/midwest/Ask-A-REL/10268

9   BIPOC: Black, Indigenous, (and) People of Color. POC is widely used as an umbrella term for all people of color, but now a different acronym is suddenly gaining traction on the internet—BIPOC, which stands for Black, Indigenous, People of Color. People are using the term to acknowledge that not all people of color face equal levels of injustice. They say BIPOC is significant in recognizing that Black and Indigenous people are severely impacted by systemic racial injustices.

—Chevaz Clarke (https://www.merriam-webster.com
/dictionary/BIPOC)s

10   Palmer, Parker. 2000. *Let Your Life Speak: Listening
        for the Voice of Vocation* (Kindle Location 77). Kindle
        Edition.

11   Calhoun, Ada. 2021. *Why We Can't Sleep: Women's
        New Midlife Crisis*. New York: Grove Press.

12   "The Clearness Committee: A Communal Approach
        to Discernment | Center for Courage & Renewal."
        n.d. Couragerenewal.org. Accessed October 13, 2023.
        https://couragerenewal.org/library/the-clearness
        -committee-a-communal-approach-to-discernment/

13   https://www.britannica.com/topic/code-switching

14   Rohr, Richard. 2009. *The Naked Now: Learning
        to See as the Mystics See*. New York: The Crossroad
        Publishing Company.

15   Goff, Bob. 2019. *Live in Grace, Walk in Love*. Nashville:
        Nelson Books (an imprint of Thomas Nelson), p. 14.

16   Niequist, Shauna. 2022. *I Guess I Haven't Learned That Yet*. Zondervan. Chapter 20.

17   Varghese, The Reverend Winnie. 2023. Recording of *Sermon—First Sunday of Advent*. December 3. https://www.stlukesatlanta.org/podcasts/sermons/